IN HIS HANDS

To: Cheryl
Thanks for your freeing
and all of your help.
Love
Bruce Lovett

IN HIS HANDS

BRUCE LOVETT

XULON PRESS

Xulon Press
2301 Lucien Way #415
Maitland, FL 32751
407.339.4217
www.xulonpress.com

Edited by Susan Lovett

Artwork by Crystian Hopper
"For Bruce. Your story is truly amazing. Thank you."
Email: crystianhopperart@yahoo.com
Instagram: Crystian Hopper Art

Printed in the United States of America.

ISBN-13: 978-1-54566-052-2

»»»

A very special thanks to my wife, Susan, who
worked tirelessly to edit <u>In His Hands.</u>
I genuinely appreciate her expertise
and assistance in making this project become
a reality.

ACKNOWLEDGMENT

»»»

I would be remiss if I didn't thank two groups of people who helped to make the writing of this book possible.

First and foremost, there is my family.........On many occasions, I have heard people ask my wife Susan, "How did you cope with all that happened over those years?" She would quickly respond, "I realized the awesome power that we have through prayer, and what it truly means to trust God in every area of your life and in the lives of your family."

So, to my wife and children, "THANK YOU for your unwavering support, patience and understanding."

The second group I would like to thank are the men and women of law enforcement with whom I worked for many years. It was their professionalism, support and friendship that helped to make possible any successes I may have achieved in my career.

»»»

This book is an autobiography dealing with the actual cases and events that transpired during the career of Bruce Lovett. Certain names of characters have been changed in order to protect the reputation, integrity, and sensitivity of certain individuals and the role they played in the book. While some of the cases are presently ongoing, all attempts were made to protect the safety and privacy of those individuals.

CONTENTS

>>>>>>

»»»

There was little time to react. His first bullet broke my left forearm and sent shrapnel all through my arm. My flashlight went flying from my hand. Within seconds I was struck three more times, even though I started firing back after his first shot.

CHAPTER 1
EARLY BEGINNINGS

»»»

It was a cool fall afternoon in 1959, when Merritt Lovett walked out on the front porch of his home in rural Choctaw, Alabama. The wind was blowing slightly, and the amber reeds of grass were bending all so gently in the pasture across the road from his house. Merritt had moved his family to Alabama the previous year when he went to work at the local paper mill as an electrician. As he stared at the herd of wild horses grazing in the pasture, something caught his eye. He noticed the slow movement of a young, tow-headed boy crawling through the tall grass in the direction of the horses. He recognized the boy as his son Bruce (whom he always called Bud.) Suddenly the boy jumped to his feet and sprinted toward a beautiful Tennessee walker and leaped on its back. The startled horse reared on its hind legs and started galloping at a fast pace across the pasture. While gripping the horse's dark red mane, Bud rode the horse for about a quarter mile. After the horse jumped over a stream, he bailed off, tumbling several times before landing on his back side on the ground. Scraped and sore, he got up off of the ground, satisfied that the adventure had been worth the trouble. With a sense of pride, Merritt Lovett shared this story with others many times over the years.

This incident may have foretold a desire on my part to spend a good portion of my life living on the edge. I had always been intrigued by my father's own adventures. As a small boy, I went down to the docks with my sister, Jill, in Fernandina Beach, Florida. We watched my father, without a breathing device and with a knife in his mouth, dive off the docks to cut loose the rigging on a sunken fishing boat. He also enjoyed deep sea diving and had a diving suit and helmet which hung on our back porch. My father was my hero. Later in life, after he passed away, it would be my Heavenly Father who would take the place of my Dad. My Heavenly Father would use the same loving instruction to guide me in the right direction when I needed Him most.

Little did I know, at an early age, what a significant role God would play in my life and in my future.

CHAPTER 2
GROWING UP

»»»

My early years were spent giving my parents plenty of reasons to worry about my activities and my safety. I had lots of fun, but having fun wasn't always in my best interest. Growing up in rural Choctaw County, Alabama, did not allow me ample opportunity for serious mischief, but there was no lack of effort on my part.

As a child growing up, I had to overcome many fears. I suppose it is not uncommon for young boys to be fearful about certain things in life, and I was no exception. I knew I must overcome these fears in order to become a man. I had a fear of darkness. I had a fear of heights, and I was afraid of older boys. I realized at an early age that if I were to conquer these fears, I would have to challenge myself and meet them head on. I was able to get over my fear of darkness by running around my house in the dark and later walking around until I saw that nothing was going to harm me. To overcome my fear of heights, I would go to a nearby fire tower and climb it, one section at a time, until I was able to go to the top of the hundred- foot tower.

When I was a young teenager, I was swimming down at the creek with some other boys when I got into an altercation with a boy three years my senior. He hit me and knocked my head against a tree. My lip was bleeding, and through the tears, I angrily told him that I wouldn't always be smaller than him, and when that day came, I would seek revenge. About three years later the day came when he was at home on leave from the army, and I was in high school. I was taller than he was by then and much stronger than I had been before. We got into another argument, and this time when the fight started, I was ready for him. After the fight I told him, "See, I told you I would get even one day, and that time is now." Now I know fighting was not the proper way to handle things, and I began to see there was no real victory in physically beating someone. I felt a degree of satisfaction, but there was remorse along with the victory. My fears were now behind me, and this would help me later in life as I challenged myself many times to overcome obstacles.

In 1959, I received my first introduction into the criminal justice system. A man in our community had been charged with murdering his wife, dumping her body down a well, and using a bulldozer to push dirt in on top of her. This family was a very prominent family in the community, as were the prosecutor and defense attorneys in the case. There was much sensationalism surrounding the trial. Although I was a young boy, my friends and I would go to the courthouse and go up in the balcony to watch and listen as the trial was going on. To my knowledge, to this day, Choctaw County hasn't had a case of that magnitude. Beginning at an early age, I developed a pattern of intrigue for the criminal justice system which would drive my decisions and shape my life.

In the early 50's and 60's, jobs in Choctaw County were scarce. Those who were not employed at the local paper mill were relegated to jobs such as farming, picking cotton, raising cows; and of course, bootlegging. At an early age, I learned when hunting and walking up on someone's still, you raise your gun over your head and back away, tracing your steps, in hopes that whoever was watching might not shoot or mistake you for a revenue agent.

My friend, Everette Schofield, and I entertained ourselves on Saturday afternoons by catching a ride on a neighbor's mule and wagon down to Hollis James' store. After buying a soft drink, we would sit on the perimeter of a vacant lot next to the store and get ready for the activities which were about to begin. You see, on some Saturdays, J.C. Jones and the Haggin brothers would arrive in an old pick-up truck. After positioning themselves on the ground in a circle, they would pass around a gallon jug of moonshine whiskey and take turns having a drink. The more they drank, the meaner and more brazen they became. While we were not close enough to hear the mumbled conversations, we knew what would eventually transpire. Suddenly one of them would get up off the ground, walk across the circle, and knock one of the others backwards with his fist. The aggressor would then return to his place in the circle, and the drinking and conversation would continue. This activity would go on for one to two hours, and Everette and I would just watch while anticipating which one would be the next victim.

Interestingly enough, after the whiskey ran out, they would all pile into the old truck, three in the front and two in the back, and leave together—all good friends. This was some of our favorite entertainment on a lazy, Saturday afternoon.

Other pastimes, when we were not doing chores or attending school, included playing in the old cotton gin, which had been closed for several years. We also played basketball in the closed, old two-story school house which was close to my home. My friend, Ronnie Gibson, had several horses on his farm, and we would ride them bareback down to the creek, which was about two miles away where we would go skinny-dipping on hot, summer afternoons.

1964 was not one of my better years growing up. I decided that high school was not very entertaining, so I would ride the school bus eighteen miles to school, check in at homeroom, and many times walk downtown and hang out at the pool hall. I would then return to school in the afternoon, go to a few classes and catch the bus back home. Mrs. Kelly, my English teacher, had required us to write a research paper that year. I didn't feel like I had the time to do this, so I found a paper which my sister, Jill, had written, inserted a new cover page, and turned it in. However, I had forgotten to remove Jill's cover page, which resulted in my being failed for the entire year in English. I actually failed everything that year.

My mother never suspected I was failing in school. I solved this problem by "borrowing" a new report card from one of my teacher's desks. I would fill in the report card, giving myself A's and B's, and take this report card home for my mother to sign. I would sign my mother's name to the real report card and return it to school. I was so proud that I was able to accomplish this. It worked like a charm until they mailed my original report card home at the end of the year. I cannot begin to describe the aftermath of that debacle!

If that wasn't enough to drive my mother crazy, one Friday night, I persuaded my parents to let me go bowling in Linden which was about thirty miles away. (This was prior to my parents finding out about my grades.) I actually never intended to go bowling. I was with four boys, all but one was two to three years older than me, and we were headed for the state line.

Choctaw County was a dry county in those days, and we started out by stopping at Sickey's at the state line where we each purchased a quart of beer. After several other stops we ended up at the Sugar Shack. I was in the back room shooting craps with some sailors when cops raided the place. I only remember one of the cops asking me, "Are you drunk, son?" All of a sudden it was lights out. I was told I took a swing at one of the officers and another hit me over the head with a slap jack. Jimmy Hurst and I spent the rest of the weekend in the Lauderdale County Jail. They did not have juvenile facilities in those days. We were in a large cell with over twenty men and only eleven beds. I remember rolling a drunk sailor out in the floor and taking his bed. I did not eat anything that weekend. It looked like pig slop to me. Someone had gotten word to my parents, and my mother finally came over on Sunday to get me out. I believe my father would have just left me there. My parents sold my dog to recover some of the bail money.

All of these events that year were significant. Consequently, I learned many lessons about life, and these experiences further emphasized that God still had His hand on my life. If He could use someone like me....... He could use anyone.

From birth I had trouble with asthma. When I finished high school, I was determined to go into the military. After receiving my draft notice, my good friend,

Robert Broadhead, and I enlisted in the Marine Corp. While walking guard duty one cold, winter night, I developed a cold and started having severe asthma. They sent me to a Navy doctor who eventually told me that because of respiratory problems, I did not need to go to the tropical climate in Vietnam. They offered me an Honorable Discharge, and I went home. My father and my girlfriend, Susan, picked me up at the bus station in Meridian, Mississippi.

For many years, I would have regrets about this, especially after I heard that out of my original platoon of seventy-two young men, a large number were killed in the first year in Vietnam. When I have gone to the Vietnam Memorial in Washington, I have always felt a sense of sadness reading the names inscribed there. And yet, God had a plan.

In 1958, my mother met and befriended the Dykes family at the local church she attended. She, of course, required me to attend. Joe Dykes had also come to Choctaw County to work at the paper mill, and our two families would soon become close friends. Our families took vacations together and visited each other frequently. Jim Dykes and I were in the same class in school and played together often. My mother probably felt Jim, who was a very good student, might have a positive influence on me. She was so wrong. I was not easily persuaded.

The best thing that came out of our relationship with the Dykes was that I met Jim's younger sister, Susan, who was two and a half years my junior. Initially, we had little interest in one another, but her transition from a tomboy into a beautiful young woman caught my attention. We began dating when she was fifteen and I was seventeen. We eventually fell in love and were married on December 28, 1968. Susan's mother was not in favor of this union for two reasons. First, she felt like Susan was too young to get married. Secondly, she was aware of my reputation. With Susan's Daddy consenting to sign for her, the wedding finally took place.

We struggled for several years as I was trying to complete my college education at Southeastern University. I worked every job I could find during those years. I worked loading box cars in a fertilizer plant, selling men's clothing, selling auto parts, painting houses, or whatever I could find, as my schedule changed with each new semester. Susan worked as a hair stylist after completing Cosmetology School in Tampa, Florida.

Our first child, Bridget, was born between my junior and senior year. Two years later, we were blessed with another daughter, Amy. Finally in 1979, our third daughter, Brooke, was born. God blessed me with a beautiful family.

My first job in law enforcement was in 1969, working as a special deputy to Sheriff Monroe Brannan in Polk County, Florida. I knew immediately that I was attracted to law enforcement. It was like putting on a new pair of gloves. It felt good, and it fit.

In 1973, we moved back to Alabama where I began work as a teacher and football coach in Mobile, Alabama. I was teaching, coaching, and driving a school bus. We were barely making ends meet. So, after a year we decided to return to Florida, where I began working as a state probation officer for the Florida Probation and Parole Commission. My office was in Lakeland, Florida, on the third floor of a building overlooking Lake Mirror.

My mother's youngest brother, Billy, was nine years older than me. In keeping with my reckless behavior in those days, Billy and I challenged one another one night. The challenge was for the two of us to go and swim across Lake Hollingsworth. Now several things made this an insane wager. Lake Hollingsworth was about three quarters of a mile wide. We had no boat to go along side. The lake was known to have alligators. It was eleven o'clock at night. Need I say anything more? Oh, did I mention that I had never swam more than a hundred yards in my life. We talked my wife, Susan, into dropping us off at Florida Southern College, and I asked her to pick us up at the Yacht Club, on the other side of the lake, in about thirty minutes. We talked as we swam, and after about thirty minutes, we found ourselves tired and out in the middle of the lake. We had two choices: stop and drown or keep swimming. We talked about a possible alligator attack as we turned on our backs to float and rest. In the quiet stillness of the pitch-black night, we drifted into each other. We both thought we had bumped into an alligator, and we screamed out like little girls. An hour and fifteen minutes after we started our adventure, we arrived at the Yacht Club. Susan panicked when we didn't show up as promised. When we walked up out of the water, we faced several angry family members including my very angry, scared wife. Once again God had protected me from myself, as He still had a plan for my life.

CHAPTER 3
MY CAREER

»»»

The early years of my career in law enforcement presented many new challenges for me and my family. Our daughter, Bridget, was only two years old when we moved back to Florida, and I began my career in full time law enforcement with Probation and Parole. After college I worked for one year as a coach and teacher before gravitating back to my first love in law enforcement. As a young, inexperienced country boy from Alabama, I was supervising a caseload of hardened criminals who never ceased to test my abilities or attempt to con me. There were many types of people who I had never before encountered. One, particular offender came into my office one day wearing tight fitting capri pants and a halter top. He had on make-up, earrings and false eyelashes. As he reached out to shake my hand, I noticed his fingernails were very long and polished candy-apple red. Reluctantly, I responded. He said, "Hello, my name is Jerry. Most people just call me Precious."

Amazingly, Jerry became one of my best parolees during that time, and I never had any problems with him. I learned from this experience that even though you may not approve of a person's appearance or lifestyle, you should not rush to judge his character.

CHAPTER 4
LIFE AS A JUVENILE OFFICER

>>>

After one year, I learned that the State of Alabama had formed a new department called the State Juvenile Probation Department. Prior to this, all juvenile probation had been handled by the Department of Pensions and Security. All counties were told to hire someone to handle their juvenile probation. I met with Mark Ezell and Tom Turner, the two Probate Judges in Choctaw and Washington Counties and negotiated a plan whereby I would supervise both counties, and each county would split the cost of my salary and benefits. At that time, I was one of only two probation officers in the State who was supervising two counties. Since this was a brand-new concept, everything seemed to be a challenge, even the smallest tasks such as developing forms for use in court.

In those days, the Probate Judge was also the Juvenile Court Judge. Since a Probate Judge was not required to be an attorney, many of the Juvenile Court Judges in the State did not have a legal background. One of my judges was also an attorney, and one was not. Both were good men and a pleasure for whom to work. Since this was all very new, there appeared to be some confusion about what my responsibilities were. I was deputized by the Sheriffs of both Counties, wore a gun and a badge, and was utilized in a number of ways by the two counties.

We lived in the town of Butler, Alabama. I will never forget my first trip to the elementary school in Butler where Miriam Heaton was the principal. Mrs. Heaton had been one of my teachers in high school, and as I walked into her office I said," Good morning Mrs. Heaton. I don't know if you remember me, but I'm Bruce Lovett, and I'm the new juvenile probation officer for the county." With a gasp, Mrs. Heaton said, "You're the what?" She paused for several seconds, and I languished in the pause which seemed like minutes. "You know what Bruce, come to think of it, that makes all the sense in the world. If there was ever anyone who came through our school system who would know about juvenile delinquency it would be you." I wasn't sure this was meant to be a compliment, but I thanked her nevertheless.

Law- enforcement in those days was very different than it is today. We were allowed to do things that some would probably want to capture on their cell phones today. The danger was just as real, but many times you were on your own, as a back-up was not readily available. We had many confrontations; therefore, the

Sheriffs of both counties hired young, strong, robust men who they felt confident had plenty of courage. It was during this time that I met and befriended Larry Martin. Larry was about my age, and was working as Chief Deputy for Choctaw County. He and I rode together frequently and experienced many adventures together. While I worked well with both sheriffs, I became good friends with Donald Lolley, who was the Sheriff of Choctaw County.

Donald would call me out each time he had a case involving a juvenile. One case that I remember very well involved a twelve-year-old boy. There were two primary communities in Choctaw County that were known for their production and sale of moonshine whiskey. This boy and his family were from one of those communities. When the Sheriff called, he said the boy had shot and killed his father, and the whole family would be at the local hospital. When I arrived, I found the boy, his mother, his uncle who was his father's brother, and two of the boy's sisters. I advised the boy of his rights, in the presence of his mother, and after waiving his rights; I began to interview him.

He stated that the family had been riding around the dirt, backroads of Choctaw County all afternoon. His mother, father and uncle were in the front, and the three children were in the back. His father and uncle were drinking moonshine and were very intoxicated. He said several times his father had stopped the truck, drug his mother out of the truck, and beat her with a limb or whatever he could find. He would then force her back into the truck and drive on down the road. The children had to witness all of this, but they had become conditioned to this sort of behavior. Once they arrived back home, the beating continued. The boy said his father suddenly decided he was going to cut his mother's throat. He said his father retrieved a knife from the pocket of his overalls, opened the blade, and was holding his mother by the hair of her head while she fought and screamed. She was down on her knees. During the struggle, his intoxicated father dropped the knife and it landed under the wood burning stove. He said he had finally had all he could take when he saw his father trying to reach for the knife from under the stove. He said he told his father to let his mother go, or he would kill him. His father declined, and proceeded to curse at him. He said he went into his father's bedroom, returned with a twelve-gauge pump shotgun, and shot his father in the chest with 00 buck shot. This was what we refer to as a killing shot with no chance of survival.

After interviewing the boy, I talked to all of the others who told the same story, including the uncle, who was apparently too fearful of his brother to take action himself. I sent the family home, and called the Sheriff to tell him that I was making a ruling of Justifiable Homicide. There was no Coroner's Inquest.

There was no Grand Jury. Everyone appeared to be satisfied, and that was the end of the case.

In southern Washington County, there is a small town called McIntosh. The first time Judge Turner sent me there into the Native American community, I was supposed to meet with a resident, who I will refer to as R.C. This was in reference to his fifteen-year-old daughter, who had run off with a boy from 'the other side of the creek.' It seems that this was very significant, in that the father had no problem with his fifteen-year-old daughter getting married, but he was upset with the fact that the boy was from a family who lived on the other side of the creek. Apparently, R.C. did not approve of this family.

Judge Turner made a statement to me before I left. He said, "Now, if someone stops you and asks what your business is, just tell them Judge Tom sent you." He reiterated, "Make sure you remember to do this!" As I traveled south toward my destination, I decided to stop and introduce myself to the McIntosh Police Chief. When I told the Chief about my mission, he told me it was not a good idea. The Chief, who was not a Native American, said he did not go into their community unless they called him. I figured that he may have just been trying to scare me, but I wasn't completely sure. He said there had been people who had gone in there and went missing— not to be seen again. Nevertheless, I made the turn at Bessie's

Kitchen, as instructed, and drove about a mile when I noticed several men in a car following me. I decided to stop at a home and ask directions. After turning into the driveway, the car behind me turned in also and blocked my exit. There were four men in the car. As I left my vehicle, I just ignored them and walked up on the porch to the front door. I knocked several times, and finally a woman came to the door...leaving the screen door closed. She said, in a very stern voice, "What do you want?" I told her Judge Tom had sent me to meet with R.C. about his daughter. Ignoring me completely, the woman opened the screen door and yelled out to the man who had let down the driver's side window, "It's O.K.! Judge Tom sent him down here to see R.C." I often wondered since that day what might have happened if I had not had Judge Tom's blessings. I met with R.C. and was able to get his reluctant daughter back home.

I became friends with many of the people in this community, and many of those friendships endure to this day. My son-in law, Kirby, came from this area, and we love and respect him and his family very much.

CHAPTER 5
PROTECTION FROM HARM'S WAY

»»»

On May 16, 1978, Dean Roberts, a Butler, Alabama, police officer was on patrol during the night shift. As was often the case, I was riding with Dean on this particular night, and Dean had just dropped me off at my house. Something happened that night which would spread fear and shock all across the rural Choctaw County like nothing anyone had seen before that time. A few minutes after Dean dropped me off at my house, he noticed a car with out-of-state plates traveling very slowly down the highway near the Choctaw General Hospital. He turned on his blue lights in order to make a traffic stop. Dean later told me he had just exited his vehicle, when the passenger of the car he had stopped jumped out with a twelve-gauge shotgun and fired, striking Dean in the shoulder. Dean was able to retrieve his weapon and fired several shots at the fleeing vehicle. We did not learn until much later that one of his rounds had gone through the trunk and struck one of the subjects in the calf of the leg. Mostly incapacitated, Dean walked to the hospital and upon entering the emergency room, passed out on the floor. Had Dean not made it to the hospital, he very likely would have bled to death on the side of the highway.

All law enforcement officers in and around Choctaw County were called out and we conducted a man hunt for the remainder of that night. Road Blocks were set up, but the vehicle was not spotted. The two suspects who were escapees from prison were very savvy in the ways of law enforcement and had only driven about five miles before they ditched their car in the woods, covered it with limbs, and waited until the next day when they were sure everyone thought they were out of the area. Then they stole another car and continued their journey. One of the suspects' fathers was in law enforcement; therefore, he knew the way cops reacted in these situations.

The next afternoon the two were spotted by an Alabama State Trooper in another stolen vehicle in the north end of Choctaw County. The trooper gave chase, and they shot out his windshield. Fortunately, he wasn't seriously wounded.

We began to discover their way of operating and felt they might still be in the area. I was riding with Deputy Ed Goldman, and we were searching the back roads on the north end of the county late that night when we came to a small church on a dirt road in a deeply wooded area. In the dew-covered grass, we could see tire impressions going around to the back of the church. Ed started to drive around the church but stopped. We discussed the fact that if they were back there, we may be going into an ambush. We decided to wait until daylight. When daylight came, we returned and found their vehicle behind the church. On two occasions and on two consecutive nights, God had protected me. It seemed that He had something else in mind for me – a plan that had not yet been clearly revealed.

The two escapees traveled through the woods during the night where they killed again and took another vehicle. They eventually made it back to Oklahoma where they shot it out with the State Police. After killing one officer and wounding another, both subjects were eventually killed.

Dean Roberts eventually recovered enough to go back to work, but had physical problems for many years to follow. Dean probably also suffered from P.T.S.D. However, none of us knew about this in those days, and it was not identified as such. I began to realize that God was protecting me, and that He had a purpose for my life.

CHAPTER 6
DEFLECTION FROM LAW ENFORCEMENT

»»»

During the next year there was a series of events that took place which altered the course of my life. This was all preempted by certain choices that I made. I believe that many of the negative things that occur in our lives are due to the choices we make. We reap what we sow.

After spending four years as Chief Juvenile Probation Officer for Choctaw and Washington Counties, I started looking for a vocation in which I could earn more money. We had two precious, little girls and Susan was about to deliver our third child.

I accepted a job with the Ezell family to work in their restaurant business. We left for Montgomery, Alabama, where I became Assistant Manager of an Ezell's Catfish Cabin Restaurant. I prayed before taking this position and made a promise to God that I would not run a restaurant which sold alcohol. This promise turned out to be one of the most significant events in my life. You see, it had very little to do with alcohol, but much more to do with a promise which I made to God. After only three months in Montgomery, Charles Ezell, one of the owners, contacted me and told me they needed a manager for their restaurant in Jackson, Mississippi. He remembered that I told him I had not wanted to sell alcohol, and I knew if I accepted, I would be expected to sell alcohol in this restaurant. Blinded by the amount of money he was willing to pay me, I accepted his offer. Charles didn't try to persuade me to accept. It was clearly my decision.

One of the lessons I learned from this was that we should always be careful about the things we promise God, as there may be consequences for breaking our promises. We moved to Jackson, Mississippi, bought a house, and I settled into my new job. Not too long after I began working, I started drinking. I reasoned that if I was going to sell it, I might as well also drink it. I began by drinking one beer while checking up at the end of the night. As time went by, the volume I drank increased. I don't believe I was doing a poor job with the management of the restaurant. We had a good business, and I was making money for the owners. The problem was that God had taken His hand off of my life, and I was floundering spiritually. My personal life began to spiral out of control.

Many negative things happened during this time, all of which were my own creation. I started having an affair with one of my employees, and this resulted in her becoming pregnant. I offer no excuses for my behavior. I had a loving, beautiful wife and three sweet, adorable daughters at home. I was a man out of control. Susan left me, took the children, and moved back to Alabama. I began drinking even more at this time. I had a disagreement with one of the owners of the restaurant, and one day Charles walked in and told me I was no longer needed. Little did he or I know, at the time, this was the best thing he could have done for me.

God already had a plan for my restoration, but I could not see that far down the road. I had cultivated friendships with several important people in Jackson during the time I was running the restaurant. I hosted a birthday party for the Lieutenant Governor. I thought surely I would be able to transition into another good job, but I was seriously mistaken. Every door I knocked on was closed. I lost my home and everything I owned except a small truck. I eventually loaded my truck with my few personal possessions left remaining and headed back to Alabama.

CHAPTER 7
THE FORTUNE TELLER

»»»

With my life spinning out of control, I began to look for answers. Even though I had not changed my life style, and was drinking a lot and had lost everything, I blamed God for my misfortune. How could He turn His back on me this way? I was unemployed, and my personal life was in the toilet. I moved back to Alabama and after doing odd jobs for several months, I was hired by my old friend, Bill Taylor, as a police officer in Jackson, Alabama. Many times, when I was not on duty, I drank.

My wife, Susan, went back to college and was also working with her mother in her Beauty Salon. I am so thankful that she was such a good mother to our children during this extremely difficult time. She often speaks about how God gave her supernatural strength and how His presence enveloped her during this time.

Since we still owned a home in Jackson, Mississippi, I had gone to meet with the realtor who finally had a buyer. It was during one of these trips that someone told me about a lady in Pearl, Mississippi, that could tell fortunes and read the future. I decided to seek her out. Like most people, I had never believed in fortune telling, but I thought, at this point, what could it hurt?

I must premise this next part by saying that I am aware that Satan gives power to certain individuals on this earth. On this day, I witnessed and became a believer of that ability. This lady was an older, French lady who lived in a very modest home in Pearl. I did not call ahead or make an appointment, but instead just showed up at her house one day. She was sweeping her carport when I arrived. I exited my vehicle, walked up to her, and asked if she could tell fortunes? She stared at me intently for several seconds and then said, "Yes, I do." I asked if she would be willing to tell mine, and she agreed.

We went into her kitchen and sat at the kitchen table. It was a table common in kitchens from the 1940's and early 1950's. It was made of durable, heavy chrome steel, and had a light red formica top. I was dressed in regular street clothes, and I made up my mind beforehand that I would listen but not provide any information. She got out a deck of regular playing cards and began to lay them out as if she were playing Solitaire. As she did this, she began to speak with a heavy French accent. She said, "I see you in a uniform. You must be in some type of law enforcement. You will be changing jobs soon, and you will still be wearing a uniform, but it will be of a different color."

She said, "I see that your wife is going to have a baby." Suddenly she paused. "No, it is not your wife who is having the baby. It is someone else." She went on to tell me that the baby was going to be a girl and that she would be very sick during the first year of her life, but she would not die. She told me many things that day which made the hair stand up on the back of my neck.

She told me I had hurt many people. She said I didn't want to hurt people, but I still did nonetheless. The last thing she told me really shook me, because she had been right about so many different things in my life. She said she saw a man, and she began to describe him. She said he had dark, curly hair and a mustache. She said I would be responsible for this man's death. This shook me from my head down to my toes. What did it all mean? When would it take place? She left me with many gaps to fill and more questions than answers. Even though she did not charge me, I thanked her, gave her some money, and started to leave. It was at this point that she said something which I thought was very unusual. She said, "Everything I have told you will happen just as I have said except for one possible exception. God has the power to change the way things will take place if he chooses to do so. However, if He does not intervene, then everything will happen just as I've said it would." I realized at that moment how much Satan acknowledges the superior power of God. I also realized all of the things she had told me referencing current events were true. I began to wonder about the future. I decided that I had more than enough to worry about, and I would just have to wait to see what happened.

My daughter April was born in the spring of that year. It was a very difficult situation for several reasons. Her mother and I were not married. I knew that this child was completely blameless, and from the first day she was born, I knew that I loved her. During the first year of her life she would become gravely ill and nearly die. I am thankful that she survived. She is an adult now and the mother of two children.

During all of this I was trying to make amends with Susan, who had separated herself from me and moved back to Alabama with our children. Susan was totally blameless in all of this, and I knew I would spend the rest of my life being sorry for the pain I had caused, both to her and to my children. I also regretted not being the father to April that she needed and deserved. What the fortune teller had spoken was continuing to come true. I seemed to be hurting everyone around me. I did not know how to repair all of the damage I had caused.

For the first time in my life I considered suicide. Everything seemed so hopeless. One day, I decided I would take my own life. I sat down on the edge of the bed with a rifle in my hands and placed the barrel in my mouth. Suddenly my phone rang and, for some unknown reason, I decided to answer it. A friend, Fred Stallworth, who was a minister, said he felt impressed by God to call and check on me. My first thought was that maybe God did care about me and my situation after all, and I realized that would have been a selfish thing to do to my family. Somehow, I had to find the strength to carry on. I put the rifle back in the closet.

CHAPTER 8
FUN AND GAMES

»»»

During my time working in Jackson, Alabama, I had many memorable experiences. Sometimes we would prank each other, and I became victimized on more than one occasion. Bill Taylor was my boss. He was, and is to this day, a very good friend. On one occasion Bill called me in to the office and handed me an arrest warrant on a man named Doe McKenzie. He said I would find Doe down at the local saw mill. Bill smiled as he handed me the warrant, and this should have given me some insight of things to come. When I got to the saw mill, I went in and introduced myself to Gene Whitehead, who was the owner of the mill. After explaining to Gene I had a warrant on Doe McKenzie, he smiled and told me I would find him right down the road on a skidder. Leaving the office, I noticed Gene and a couple of other men were standing at the front window of the office watching my activity and commenting to each other while laughing. All of this unusual behavior was indicative of things that were about to transpire. After arriving at the skidder and yelling out to Doe to come down, he shut down the engine and jumped to the ground. With a less than friendly demeanor, he asked me what I wanted from him. I told him I had a warrant for his arrest. His immediate response was, "They must not have told you about me?" After explaining that no one had told me anything, he began to question me. He asked if I knew Don Lolley and Larry Linder. After telling him I was acquainted with both, he wanted to know if the two of them or Bill Taylor had told me about him. I explained that they had not, at which point he started to relate the following. He stated that he had been arrested on many occasions, but that he never went to jail without a fight. He told me the only way I was going to arrest him was if I whipped his a__ first. After quickly thinking about how I would handle this, I told him I would agree to the conditions, but I added one caveat. I told him I would fight him fairly, but he needed to know I had decided a long time ago that I would not allow any man to whip my a__, and at the moment I determined I was losing the fight, I would pull my revolver and shoot him graveyard dead. Doe stood there and stared at me intently for a few moments and then said," You serious ain't you?" I told him I was completely serious, but it wouldn't be a problem unless I started losing the fight. At this point he turned and walked to my patrol car, opened the back door and entered the car. As he did this, I heard him mumble, "You done took all the fun out of it."

Bill Taylor and I would laugh many times over the years at this incident and many others. These light-hearted moments during my career served as a buffer from the more serious events which I encountered on a daily basis and helped to mitigate the many tragedies that would occur.

CHAPTER 9
STARTING OVER AGAIN IN FLORIDA

»»»

My dad called me and told me there was an opening in the Inverness, Florida, office with State Probation and Parole. I remembered the words of the fortune teller and thought to myself, "Well, I might be changing jobs, but I will not be wearing a different colored uniform," as she had said. Perhaps this would give Susan and me a chance to start over again. I missed my family so much and longed to have them near me again. I didn't know if she could forgive me for all I had done, but I knew I loved her deeply. I really wanted my family back. It was only by the grace of God that Susan had not already made the decision to divorce me.

I arrived in Inverness, went through the interview process, and was all set to go to work. I received a call from one of the supervisors with Probation and Parole, and he informed me that they still intended to hire me, but I would be working in the city of Orlando instead of Inverness. I didn't want to move to Orlando and work in the City. I was devastated. What would

I do now? It is important to remember that God has a divine plan. We cannot see things down the road as He directs them, but we know He is in control of everything that touches our lives. God had a plan. I began working a temporary job at Florida Power while waiting on something else to materialize. Many months after arriving in Florida, Susan and the girls joined me, and she agreed to try and salvage our marriage and give me another chance. Thank God for restorations. Thank God for second chances.

CHAPTER 10
THE CITRUS COUNTY SHERIFF'S DEPARTMENT

»»»

My brother-in-law mentioned to me that Citrus County had a new Sheriff. I went to the Sheriff's Department, walked in without an appointment, and asked to speak to the sheriff. I was escorted in and introduced to Charlie Dean. Charlie Dean was a big man, about six foot five, with a very commanding and sometimes intimidating voice. I decided to be very forthright in my presentation to him. I said, "Sheriff, my name is Bruce Lovett, and I desperately need a job." He asked me a few questions and then said, "Okay, you're hired. When can you start?" I was so thankful to Sheriff Dean, and we remain friends to this day. I was now back in law enforcement. Once again, what had been predicted had occurred. I was now wearing a green uniform instead of a blue one.

Since I had moved from Alabama to Florida, it became necessary for me to attend the law enforcement academy. This was accomplished at the Withlacoochee Vocational School where the Academy was located.

Tom Kern was the Director. He later hired me as an instructor while I was working for the Sheriff's Department. I made many friends during this training, but the one that I became closest to was a man named John Luc. John was a Chief Petty Officer in the Coast Guard in Yankee Town, and after retiring, he eventually went to work for the Sheriff's Department as head of the marine unit. Any training exercises that required us to partner, John and I would always be together.

I will never forget on the night when we were doing building searches, each group that proceeded us had at least one of the cops getting shot. We were supposed to ascertain whether an individual we encountered was a good guy or a bad guy and take appropriate action. Before we did our exercise, I looked at John and said, "Look, we are going to shoot everybody as soon as we see them." We did this, and afterward the lead instructor said "You two shot everybody, including one good guy." My response was "Yeah, and we're both still alive." He just laughed at this. We knew this was just training. In real life officers are forced to make many life and death decisions throughout their career. They know that making a bad choice may cost them or someone else their life. What an incredible responsibility!

I enjoyed the life of a deputy sheriff. There was always a new challenge with every shift I worked. Living on the edge seemed to fit my personality. I was intrigued by the opportunity to figure things out

THE CITRUS COUNTYSHERIFF'S DEPARTMENT

and solve crimes that I discovered as I responded to calls. There were also numerous opportunities to help people who could not help themselves.

I once received a call for assistance at a golf course where an elderly man had been struck by lightning. Upon my arrival, I discovered he was not breathing. I immediately began to administer CPR, and after a couple of minutes, he began breathing on his own. However, before the EMT's arrived, he stopped breathing again. I again started CPR and continued until emergency personnel arrived. Upon their arrival, they took over and transported him to the hospital. The man lived and survived for three more years before dying of natural causes. This was just one of many situations, and it was not uncommon for all of us who were primary responders during that time. I witnessed many courageous acts by many of my comrades during those days. Many of the things we did were never publicized, but we had a very strong support group within our ranks, and a very close relationship. We had to depend upon each other and always had each other's backs. We sometimes argued and disagreed, but we knew when things got ugly, we could depend on each other for support.

I had also been chosen to be a member of the CERT (Citrus Emergency Response Team). I was very excited about being a SWAT team member.

A deputy Sheriff in a county the size of Citrus must deal with many situations.....most of the time on their own. I remember one call I received which was originally described as a domestic situation. Upon my arrival at the mobile home in the Crystal River area, a woman met me at the door with a very worried look on her face. She invited me into the living room where I observed a man sitting on the couch holding a butcher knife. Also, in the middle of the floor was a baby in a playpen. I persuaded him to put the knife down on the kitchen table and started to engage him in conversation. He informed me he was from royal lineage and he received direction from the Queen of England. When I asked him how he received his direction from the queen, he said she spoke to him through a floor fan on a pedestal. I asked him if he could actually hear her voice through the fan, and in a matter of fact manner, he told me if I would put my ear close to the fan, I could also hear the voices. I asked him what type of instruction he had received from the Queen, and he told me she told him to kill the infant in the playpen. I knew if I rushed him there was a possibility he may be able to harm his wife and the child should I not successfully overtake him. I was aware he was experiencing severe psychosis. Therefore, I wanted to avoid shooting him. I made an excuse that I wanted my buddy to hear the voices coming out of the fan also. This gave me an opportunity to call for a backup.

I then proceeded to engage him in conversation until another deputy arrived.

Upon his arrival, I explained to him about the voices coming from the fan and how the voices had instructed him to kill the small child. At this point, we rushed him and wrestled him to the floor and were able to handcuff him. After explaining to his wife what our plans were, I told her he would be Baker Acted for a period of seventy-two hours. At this point, he would either be released or remanded to the custody of a State Mental Hospital. It was my feeling that he would probably remain in the custody of a psychiatric unit, but informed her she should take her child to a safe environment and seek legal assistance. As law enforcement officers, we were constantly involved in situations wherein deadly force might be necessary. We always tried to avoid this….especially where individuals may not be responsible for their actions.

Susan, the children and I were living in the Floral City Community. This was a rural area of south Citrus County in Florida. We were in an area surrounded by sand and scrub oaks. My daughters, Bridget and Amy, were attending Floral City Elementary School and our youngest, Brooke, was in daycare. Susan was working for the Hagar Agency (an insurance agency) in nearby Inverness, Florida, and also working as a real estate agent for Kiser Realty. We had once again settled into a normal lifestyle, or so we thought.

CHAPTER 11
THE SHOOTOUT

》》》

I must preface the things I am about to account by saying this: Those who do not believe in the supernatural ability of God may not believe, and may discount these incidents as being fabrications and/or literary sensationalism. I can only tell what I know to be true, and stand by what I am about to reveal.

It was a hot, muggy day on August 16, 1983, when an occurrence took place that would alter my life and the lives of my family forever. Susan was at work, and I was home with the children. Even though we had reconciled our marriage over the previous three years, I had still been unable to completely reconcile my relationship with God. I felt extremely distant from God. Although I was attending church with my family, I was only going through the motions. I had not allowed God to be an integral part of my life. I was to work the evening shift as a patrol deputy with the Sheriff's Department that day and remembered suddenly feeling a pervasive oppression coming over me and surrounding me like a cloud. I felt like there must be something terribly wrong, and I did not know or understand this strange feeling. I told the children to continue playing as I went into my room to lay down for a while before going to work.

As I closed the door and laid across the bed, I began to talk to God for the first time in several years. I said, "God, why am I feeling this way, and what is wrong? You know I have tried serving you and I just can't live a Christian life. I have failed you so many times, and in so many ways." At this point God started to answer me. It was not an audible voice, but He spoke directly and clearly to my heart. Now many may say, "How do you know it was God?" I can only say, when you are a child and your earthly father calls your name, you may not see him, but you recognize his voice. In this case, I knew this was the voice of my Father. He said, "Bruce, your problem is that you think you can do everything on your own, but you can't. The only way you will ever be able to serve me is if you relinquish control, and allow me to do it through you." I responded, "God, you know how weak I am, and how many times I have tried to live right, and still failed." I said, "Nevertheless I surrender myself to you, and acknowledge you as my Lord. I will try, but I must have your help in order to do this." At this point, God said something to me I did not fully comprehend. He said, "You must go through something very serious, but know this I will be with you during that time." The cloud had now lifted from over me, and the perplexing oppression was gone.

What had just occurred was something for which I had no logical explanation. How do you explain to other people that you have had a visitation from the spirit of God? What did it all mean? The only thing I did know was that I must try to live a better life, and allow God to help me and give me strength. This would not be easy, and there would be many struggles many times over the years. I knew I must try, and depend completely on God in my times of weakness.

It was a warm, Tuesday afternoon when I reported for work at three o'clock that day. Ed Owens was a twenty-year-old Explorer with the Sheriff's Department whom I had befriended. The young man had asked if he could ride with me that evening. Most of the shift had involved mostly routine calls and writing several reports.

At eleven o'clock, we had checked out at the Crystal River Police Department, and as my shift came to an end, we were talking to the dispatcher when the phone rang. She told me the call was for me. The voice on the phone was my dispatcher who told me they had one more call holding, and all of the other deputies were on other calls. She asked if I would mind taking one more call before ending my shift. I told her I would. She said the complainant would be driving a red pick-up truck and he would be waiting on me beside the highway in the Citronelle community. She said it was a prowler call. We proceeded to Citronelle and talked with the complainant, and the following information was provided. He said he lived in the mini farms area off of Dunklin Street. He said his dogs had been barking at something up the hill from his house. He said the double wide mobile home on the property had been vacant for weeks, and he wondered if someone might be in there. We followed him to the location and while he went back to his residence, we went to the mobile home where he had directed us.

Upon arrival, I shined my spotlight on the front of the structure and told Ed to stay with the car. I checked the front door which was locked, and with flashlight in hand, went around to the back. When I walked up on the faded, wooden back porch and checked the door, it was also locked. Noticing what appeared to be jimmy marks on the lock, my suspicion was somewhat aroused. I went back around to the front and stood on my tip toes in my black boots so I could see into the front living area. Although the house was vacant, I could see the tops of someone's knees who was apparently asleep on the living room floor. I immediately returned to my car and was attempting to call for back-up when I noticed Ed had left the car and was walking toward the mobile home. I yelled, "Ed, get back away from there." This apparently woke the man inside and he stood up in front of the window. I told him to get his hands in the air, as I drew my weapon. In those days we were issued a Smith and Wesson 357 Magnum revolver with semi-jacketed, 158 grain ammunition. Upon my order, he bolted for the back door. I ran around the mobile home, and as he ran out on the back porch, I once again drew down on him and in a demanding manner, told him to get his hands in the air, and that he was under arrest. He looked at me with cold dark eyes and jumped off the porch running for the woods. I gave chase while holstering my weapon.

At this point, I did not have probable cause to inflict deadly force. All I could do was chase him. We ran about fifty yards into the woods and at a clearing, he tripped and fell. Once again, I told him to get his hands in the air. He was lying on the ground, facing me, propped up on his elbows. He sat up, started to raise his hands; and as he did this, apparently pulled a pistol from his belt and started to fire. There was little time to react. His first bullet broke my left forearm and sent shrapnel all through my arm. My flashlight went flying from my hand. Within seconds I was struck three more times, even though I started firing back after his first shot.

I could not see him after I lost my flashlight, so I just fired at his muzzle flash. As I had fired all six of my rounds, I dropped to my knees to reload. With my left forearm shattered, my hand would not work properly. Attempting to reload with a speed loader, I dropped my bullets on the ground. It was at this point when I saw him in the dense moonlight getting up from the ground. HAD I NOT EVEN HIT HIM? He was standing there facing me with his gun in his hand. We were only about twenty-five feet apart. My gun was empty. I was shot in both legs, my groin and my arm. Running away was not an option, and I don't believe that it would have been anyway. That's not my nature. Thoughts raced wildly through my mind...... If he has a bullet left, he is going to come over here and finish me off, would I be able to spring from the ground when he gets closer, dive into him, try to get my good hand on his throat, choke him? What could I do? There was not adequate time to think and absolutely no time to plan! Under the circumstances, I would do whatever ....whatever was necessary to survive!

Suddenly, it happened. I felt a feeling like I had never felt before. It was like God had reached down from Heaven and wrapped His hand around me. There is no greater feeling than knowing you are IN HIS HANDS. The feeling is totally indescribable. There was a glow coming from over my head, and whatever it was, Strickland was seeing it. I picked up my flashlight and was shining it on him when I saw his eyes getting bigger and bigger. He was terrified over what he saw and began to stagger backwards. He started to walk off into the woods, and at the edge of the clearing he paused and looked back at me. What must he have been thinking? I can only imagine the thoughts that raced through his mind as he had encountered what must have been an angel of God possibly with sword drawn, hovering over me, and filling him with the fear I saw reflected in his eyes. He then slowly staggered off into the woods. I remember saying out loud as this was taking place, "Father, I feel your presence." I got up from the ground, gathered my weapon and bullets, and started walking back toward my patrol car. Giving chase was no longer an option for me.

When I got to the back yard, the complainant had pulled his truck around the house into the back yard. I climbed up into the bed of the truck and told him to take me to the hospital. At this point, I heard another shot. Laying on my back with my gun secured between my knees, I successfully reloaded. I then took a posi- tion looking over the edge of the bed, as I thought he was shooting at me again. I was ready to return fire.

There were no other shots. The complainant told me his wife was alone at his house, so I told him to return home, lock all of the doors, and arm himself. I told him not to come out until someone from law enforcement came to his door.

I asked Ed to drive me to the hospital. The poor boy was so upset that he wiped out several ditches along the way. A large number of City, County and State law enforcement personnel responded to the scene. My swat team was there, and with a search dog; they began to track Strickland. They found him about one hundred yards from where the shootout occurred. He was sitting next to a large pine tree and had been bleeding profusely from the four shots I had returned that found their target. He had made comments to other people that he would not be taken alive. With his last bullet, (yes, he did have one bullet left in his gun); he shot himself in the head.

James Dennis Strickland was thirty-eight years old when he died. He had been convicted of murder in 1973, bank robbery in 1978, and was wanted for a murder he had committed two months prior to this incident and an armed robbery just two days before. I was told he was on the U.S. Marshalls' most wanted list. His list of arrests throughout his life was extensive. He was described as a cold-blooded killer who would kill over practically anything.

When I arrived at the hospital, the hospital staff was already waiting for me. They began to cut my bloody uniform off and started giving me shots for the pain. It was reported I was shot five times, but later determined to be four—which was PLENTY! He was using a Charter Arms 38, Caliber five shot revolver. The confusion was over the fact that I had five entry wounds. One of the bullets had gone through my scrotum, exited and then went into my left leg. I had apparently turned to the side when he started firing, or some of the bullets may have been deflected by a higher power. There were three surgeons who operated on me throughout the night: one to repair and cast my broken left arm, one to repair the damage to my groin area, and a general surgeon which was taking out the bullets and putting in drainage tubes. At four o'clock the next day, they took me back into surgery. The surgeon told Susan there was a bullet lodged right next to the main artery in my left leg. He said if that bullet had been a fraction further over, I probably would have bled to death before reaching the hospital.

Even in this situation, God was in complete control. While He allowed me to be hit multiple times, He made sure all of the bullets were not into vital organs.

CHAPTER 12
THE AFTERMATH

»»»

I was in the hospital for ten days. After about four days, I started to refuse the shots of Demerol. When I began to look forward to them with a sense of anticipation, I realized this could be harmful for me, and it was time to stop taking them. It was difficult dealing with the media. There were television cameras outside my door and reporters asking for interviews. Not wanting to appear rude, I would smile for pictures and try to be gracious during interviews, but the entire time I was very uncomfortable with all of the attention. I would wonder to myself, didn't I just cause the death of someone, and now I'm everybody's hero. I thought about Strickland's children, his parents and his ex-wife. I wondered how they must be feeling and what thoughts were going through their minds.

On the fourth day I received a phone call which, after being screened, I was told I needed to take. The lady identified herself, and I did not know who she was. She began to tell me a story. She said she was the mother of three children, and her husband was a contractor. She said two months ago her husband had gone to meet his foreman at a lounge in Pompano Beach to discuss a job they were working on. She said her husband was a very large man, about six feet four inches and weighed over two hundred pounds. She told me her husband's foreman was a black man. She went on to say that while the two of them were talking in the almost empty lounge, a man approached them and said to her husband, "What are you doing with that nigger in here?" Her husband told him to mind his own business, and that they were not bothering anyone. He persisted and caused enough problems that the bartender finally told him he had to leave. The man went outside and waited at his vehicle until the two men came out of the lounge. At this point he approached her husband and asked, "Are you ready to finish that argument now?" With the same gun he had used to shoot me, he shot her husband four times in the chest killing him instantly. He then walked casually back to his vehicle and left the scene. The murderer was later identified as James Dennis Strickland.

She expressed her appreciation by saying, "Thank you for stopping him before he had a chance to kill someone else's husband and leave their children without a father." These words of reassurance and thanks would help me very much during the coming months and years.

As I lay in the hospital, the words of the fortune teller continued to resonate over and over in my mind. Her description of James Dennis Strickland was completely accurate. Another thing she said was that I would be responsible for his death, not that I would kill him. With this incident now over, all of the things she had predicted had finally come true, and I could now put to rest this chapter in my life. Or at least, I would try............

CHAPTER 13
P.T.S.D.

»»»

I n 1983, I had never heard of Post-Traumatic Stress Disorder. If anyone in the Sheriff's Department knew anything about it, they never mentioned it to me.

Almost two weeks had passed since the shooting, and I was home from the hospital recuperating. I had not been offered any counseling or therapy. That just wasn't the way it was done in those days. I suppose a man was just supposed to be a man and handle it.

It was a warm September night in Florida, and the air conditioner was running. I was lying in bed with my arm still in a cast and my legs heavily bandaged. Susan was asleep, and as I lie awake, many thoughts were racing through my mind. A cold sweat enveloped my body and I became very anxious. Suddenly I heard dogs barking outside of the house. He's back I thought to myself. I have to go out and protect my family. I must finish this. Getting out of the bed, I retrieved my pistol from the shelf in the top of the closet, and with nothing on but my underwear, I prepared myself for another shoot-out. Susan had awakened during my preparation and asked what was wrong? I simply said. "He's back." I'm sure she thought I had lost my mind, but because of my persistence, and since there was a loaded gun in my hand, she just waited patiently to see how everything played out. She didn't want to wake up the children and scare them or place them in any kind of danger. I headed out the front door with my flashlight in one hand and my weapon in a combat ready position. Moving stealthily around the house, I anticipated the next shootout. Suddenly I realized what I was doing. Strickland was dead. There were no armed adversaries in my yard. There was no imminent danger. My family was safe. Returning to the house, I tried to explain something to Susan which I did not fully understand myself.

It would be years later before I would have a name for what I was experiencing. It was PTSD (Post Traumatic Stress Disorder.) From time to time I still have nightmares and problems to this day, but like most men, I tried to handle it.

I went back to work about two weeks after the shootout. My legs were still bandaged and my arm was in a sling, but I felt like I must challenge myself and face this head on; otherwise I might never be able to continue my law enforcement career. Doing this, I learned, would not be an easy task.

On one occasion, I was riding back from Inverness to our home late one night, when I heard a call that there was a man with a gun inside of a bar in Floral City. I had just passed the bar, so I turned around and went back. Upon entering, customers pointed to the man, and I was able to take him into custody and remove the gun without any problems. After handcuffing him, we waited outside for other deputies to arrive. Upon their arrival one of the deputies said to me, "Are you alright?" I asked, "Why?" and he told me I was white as a sheet and sweating profusely. During all of the excitement, I hadn't even noticed. I knew it would be sometime before I would be able to function normally again. Sometimes I wondered how long it would take for me to return to normal and what would normal really be?

CHAPTER 14
ACCOLADES

≫≫≫

In December of 1983, the Citrus County Sheriff's Department presented me with two medals and commendations: a medal for being wounded in the line of duty, and the medal of valor. The Citrus County Commission presented me with a resolution for outstanding service in the line of duty. I received a certificate for induction into the Legion of Honor at the National Police Hall of Fame. I am revealing all of this, because I received all of this recognition because I shot someone four times. While I sincerely appreciated all of the attention and recognition, I felt badly that it was all for this reason. Had I not saved many lives in the past and yet hardly anyone knew and very few even cared. Oh well, I suppose this is the nature of the business.

After going back to work, I knew there would be several questions that would have to be answered. How would I respond the next time I got into a, "Shoot, don't shoot situation?" Would I shoot too quickly in anticipation of being shot again, or would I hesitate and have it cost me my life, or the life of someone else? Those who criticize the split-second decisions of law enforcement have no concept of the heavy burden they carry with them every time they put on a uniform and advise they are 10-8, (on duty and available for calls.)

CHAPTER 15
ADJUSTING TO LIFE AFTERWARDS

>>>>

Jim Melrose was the SWAT team commander, and he had served in the Marine Corp. On this particular day the SWAT team was having a training exercise where we were to take an abandoned house. With my arm still in a sling, I had agreed to act as a bad guy inside the house. As we were walking down the wooded path to the house, Jim was walking behind me. Suddenly, and without warning, he fired a round from a 12-gauge shotgun into the ground just behind me. The hair stood up on the back of my neck, and immediately I felt the horror of what had taken place only three weeks prior to this. I turned to Jim and calmly said, "Why did you do that?" Jim said it was a test to make sure I would be able to handle being around gunfire and not panic. Angrily, I told him never to do that again! Jokingly I said, "If you do, I may have to shoot you."

My life had mostly calmed down, and I was trying very hard to get things back to normal. The Sheriff's Department had decided to focus in a somewhat different area. We were being inundated with thefts and home burglaries. The department formed a Street Crimes Unit. This was a unit made up of four men; Jim Cernich, John Hemmer, Don King and me. Initially, Don King was Sergeant over the unit. Our job was to proactively anticipate and investigate thefts and burglaries in the County. We were very successful, solving many burglaries and thefts, and recovering thousands of dollars in stolen property. I was starting to realize that God was directing me in this work. Many times, I prayed to myself about different cases, and God would direct me to a particular location or place me strategically where I needed to be in order to solve the case. It likely appeared to others that I was simply doing a great job, but I knew who was giving me insight and direction. Many times, throughout our lives, if we could only turn our situations and problems over to God, we would start to see His hand directing us and steering us in the right direction. When we do this, He will begin to show us his favor and give us the direction we need to accomplish His will for our lives.

After a while Don left the unit and went back into patrol. We worked as a team and accomplished much during this time.

CHAPTER 16
THE PAWN SHOP

»»»

The sheriff hired an undercover officer from Pinellas County, and the four of us attempted something which had not been done before in our County. We rented a single-wide mobile home and modified it slightly. The undercover who we had hired went by the name J.R. We had one large room with a chest high counter at one end of the room. On the counter was a car radio speaker. Inside of the speaker we had placed a microphone. On the wall behind the counter we hung a mirror. This mirror was actually a two-way mirror, and we had a video camera set up on a tripod in the next room so we could video any exceptional transactions that might take place through a hole we had created in the wall. Business cards were placed around the edge of the mirror to give the surroundings more of a legitimate look. The four of us had all grown beards and had settled into our new home away from home. We had shelves on which we stocked unclaimed property from the Sheriff's Department along with property of our own which we no longer needed. J.R.'s Pawn Shop was finally open for business.

Now that we were working under cover, it became imperative that each member of our unit adopt a different name. I chose a name which had belonged to two of my forefathers and I went by the nick-name my parents had given me, "Bud." I had a legitimate Florida driver's license under this name; and we became, when we were working, these individuals. It was difficult living two different lives at the same time and keeping the two separate. It was especially difficult during this time trying to maintain a strong relationship with God. We spent many hours hanging out in bars at night trying to perpetuate the characters we had become. I never stopped praying, and I never stopped seeking God's guidance in my life.

At night J.R. circulated among the many night spots in the area trying to drum up business. It did not take long before business came calling. Word was out on the street that we would purchase drugs, stolen property or a combination of the two. We actually ran it as a pawn shop in that we purchased property that wasn't stolen and took a few pawns just to make sure everything appeared legitimate. We made customers show proof of identification so we could later include this in the arrest warrants. We videotaped every transaction to use as evidence in court. We were having a lot of fun and making many cases.

On several occasions, we had law enforcement personnel come to the pawn shop to look around. When they pulled up out front, we simply locked the door and would not let them in. This aggravated them, and they would usually leave in a huff. This was done, because early on, a decision was made that only a handful of the higher ups in the Sheriffs' Department knew about our operation. Our families were only given limited information. We knew the less people who knew; the greater chance for success.

We had several situations to occur which were quite humorous:

One day, a man, who I will refer to as Paul, came in to sell us psilocybin mushroom extract. This was a natural, hallucinogenic drug derived from a particular mushroom which, in addition to creating feelings of euphoria, can also cause poisoning and/or death. We only transacted these deals after waiting for other customers to leave and locking the door. On one of these occasions, Paul was standing at the counter and was looking up at the mirror when he thoughtfully said, "Do you guys remember the movie with Burt Reynolds and Dom Delouse where the cops were running a pawn shop and they had a video camera behind a mirror, and they videotaped all of the drug and property deals?" I said, "Yea, I seem to remember that Paul." He said, "Well I was wondering if maybe you guys might be doing the same thing?" We all just laughed, and I slid the car speaker closer to him and said, "You've got us Paul. Just speak louder so the hidden mic will pick you up." Paul thought this was very funny, and we all had a good laugh. The whole time we were videotaping the transaction, and the mic inside the car speaker was picking him up very clearly.

For over six months we continued to run the pawn shop. Others in the Sheriff's Department were told we were on assignment outside the county. We continued to purchase stolen property, marijuana, cocaine and various other drugs. We had all of the comforts of home. We took turns cooking our own meals and watched television in a back bedroom. We did just enough legal business to continue to look legitimate, but our main business was setting up bad guys. It was amazing how they kept coming in. Word was out on the street. J.R.'s was the place to do business. We didn't have to resort to entrapment, they came to us. We learned, in most instances, we didn't have to masquerade what we were doing. The people we were dealing with were not exactly rocket scientists. I remember one guy came in, and our conversation went like this.

He said, "Would you be interested in buying a 30-30, rifle?"

"I might," I said, "but if it's hot, you need to tell me. I have a way of moving it outside the county, and I don't want to get caught with it. They would close me down."

"Oh, it's hot alright. I just boosted it this past week-end," he said.

"Bring it on in," I said. "I think we can do business." Even though the owner of the gun may not have been able to provide a serial number when he reported the burglary, knowing when it was taken made it easy to track down the owner and verify that it was indeed stolen property. These types of conversations were very normal and the four of us took turns arranging transactions during that time.

Another interesting character who we did business with, I will only refer to as Mike. Mike bagged up small baggies of marijuana and brought them to us in a shoe box. We would pick up the baggies so the video could plainly identify the contents, and after haggling over the price, we would purchase several bags. Our business with Mike made for an interesting arrest on the last day we were in business. We had to formulate a plan for closing the business and arresting the suspects.

CHAPTER 17
THE PLAN

»»»

After much discussion and preparation, we had determined how we were going to shut down the pawn shop, and the day we were going to do this. We decided on the last day, we would make appointments with as many of the clients as we could and schedule them about fifteen minutes apart. Much preparation had already taken place including; identifying each of the suspects, running a criminal history and current warrants search, obtaining an arrest warrant, and in some cases, a search warrant in order to find additional stolen property and/ or drugs. The plan was such that whenever a suspect arrived, we would buy additional drugs or stolen property from them, arrest them, and take them into the back room to be processed. We would then take them out the back door to an awaiting unmarked vehicle and take them off to jail while we waited for the next suspect to arrive. As you can imagine, this required a lot of strategic planning as well as timing. Since most criminals are not necessarily punctual, we were forced to come up with some alternative plans in order to pull this off. We would have a suspect arrive early, and we would meet them at the door and tell them we were currently doing a drug deal inside and get them to come back. Other times one might arrive late and we would reschedule them to come back, because we already had someone on the way. It was amazing how well everything fell into place.

I will never forget when Paul arrived that day, we purchased some drugs from him and then I said, " Hey Paul, do you remember the day when you said you wondered if this might be an undercover operation, and that the mirror on the wall might be a two-way mirror with a video camera behind it?" As I finished saying this we reached behind the counter and were putting on our Sheriff's Department caps and pulling our guns. "Well Paul, you were right." It was a classic moment seeing the blood drain from Paul's face. He was completely speechless for several moments.

To say everything went perfectly that day, would be an understatement. It went about as close to perfect as we could have hoped for.

We knew once word got out, some of the family and friends of the arrested might decide to burn down the pawn shop; so, we were forced to close the shop and remove all of the property the same day. At the end of the day we had a Ryder truck backed up at the pawn shop, and we were all, (investigators from C.I.D.), removing the contents. Each of us were wearing a badge, a cap and a jacket, identifying who we were. While we were loading everything up, our old friend Mike pulled up. When we approached the car, Mike said, "What are y'all doing?" I said, "We are going out of business Mike. We are closing up the shop." Sgt. Henry Wilkins overheard the conversation and walked over to our location. Mike said "I thought you might want to buy some weed." Thus, Mike opened up a shoe box revealing a number of quarter ounce bags of marijuana. Henry asked, "Do you think you have enough for all of us?" With this, Mike began to count all of the investigators who were now staring at him and thinking, is this guy for real? He then counted the number of baggies in the shoe box and proclaimed, "Yes, I think I have enough." Henry then told Mike he would buy all he had. He asked Mike if he would accept gold as payment. "Gold," Mike said, "What do you mean?" Henry then produced his badge from his belt and showed it to Mike. "That's a cop's badge." Mike stated. At which point Henry said, "That's right, and we are all cops." Henry opened the door to Mike's car, and Mike fell out on the ground and started pounding the sand with his fist and crying profusely. Henry, always being the comedian, lay down on the ground next to Mike and patted him on the shoulder trying to reassure him. Henry told him it wasn't so bad, "Lots of people get arrested. You are not the first one." At this point Mike said, "I can't believe that you have lied to another human being." With this, we were all laughing so hard we could hardly contain ourselves. These humorous moments we shared always seemed to take the edge off of unusually tense situations in which we often found ourselves.

The final outcome from the pawn shop operation was that more than thirty people were arrested on over one hundred felony charges. Charlie Dean was running for reelection as Sheriff at the time, and although the pawn shop operation had nothing to do with politics, the outcome certainly helped to solidify the race for Sheriff Dean!

CHAPTER 18
THE TRANSITION

»»»

P rior to this time our unit had been known as the Street Crimes Unit (SCU). After the pawn shop, we began to transition into a more diversified unit which worked all types of special investigations; including, but not limited to, narcotics. The Citrus County Sheriff's Department had not, before that time, had an entire unit devoted to these types of crimes. Our name was changed to the Special Investigations Unit (SIU). Sheriff Dean did not particularly like using the word special in the name, but the name was not indicative of the people in it, but rather the types of investigations we conducted. We were working Special Investigations as opposed to General Investigation. The unit initially consisted of Mike Imperial, Jim Cernich, John Hemmer, me and others who transitioned in and out including Jerry Thompson, Reuben Garcia and Jack Schliep. John eventually left to enter private business, and Jerry Thompson transferred into General Investigation. I had been promoted to Sergeant and was charged with leading the unit. There are many adjectives I could use to describe this time in the unit; exciting, adventuresome, dangerous, but most of all it was lots of fun. In those days we were trying to blend in to the drug culture with which we were dealing. We all had long hair, a beard and wore sleeveless tee-shirts. We wore a shoulder holster which was concealed under a cotton sport coat. We each had a Florida Driver's license under the name we had given ourselves and sometimes went by nicknames. My nick- name was Bud. We did a lot of work with informants and undercover operatives. We bought drugs, sold drugs in reverse stings and worked cases with those who were involved in organized crime and associated with the drug culture. We worked a lot of cases with D.E.A and U.S. Customs. We were living every young law enforcement officer's dream.

CHAPTER 19
PORT PARADISE

»»»

W orking narcotics undercover was both exciting and challenging. I found myself looking forward to going in to work each day. We never knew what exciting challenge we might be faced with, and we enjoyed putting bad guys in jail. We faced danger every time we left the house, but we were having fun, and we were making a difference.

We worked many drug cases during those days. Sometimes we played the part of Bad Guys and make deals ourselves, and sometimes we used informants. On this particular occasion we had set up a drug buy with two bad guys who were in a room at the Port Paradise Motel. We had networked with many individuals in the lounge of the motel on previous occasions. This time we used an informant to make a buy from the two bad guys in one of the rooms. The drug we had purchased was powdered cocaine. There were some specifics that had to be worked out prior to taking them down. Both of the men were known to be armed, and there was a woman and two children in the room. The room was located on the second floor, and with the cooperation of management we were able to secure a room right next door. All rooms were accessed from the outside. Utilizing a listening device, we were able to listen somewhat through the wall. We decided we needed to have separation between the two bad guys and so we waited for one of them to leave the room. When we heard him leaving, we came out of our room pretending to leave at the same time. As we walked past, we turned and jumped the man and wrestled him to the concrete. We found a small pistol in his pocket. We cuffed him and one of our guys took him to the car. Using a room key which we took out of his pocket, we unlocked the door. As we did this, we heard the distinct sound of a semi-automatic rifle being chambered. Swinging the door open, we saw a man, completely naked, sitting on the bed with an M-1 .30 Cal rifle in his hands. The woman and two children were hovering directly behind him. The rifle appeared to have a thirty-round clip, but he had not yet pointed it at us.

Many times, law enforcement officers are forced to make split second decisions that could cause the death of the officers and/ or the innocent people around them. We ordered him to drop the weapon several times, but he did not respond. I knew if gunfire erupted, we could be killed, the suspect could be killed and more importantly an innocent woman and her two small children could be killed. I told Jim and Mike to cover me and I walked toward the man with my 9 mm pointed at his head. I figured if I had to shoot, I would make a head shot and hope the woman and kids would not get hit. When I got close enough, I reached out and grabbed the rifle barrel with my left hand, and struck the bad guy across the side of his head with my firearm, knocking him to the floor. We placed him under arrest and when we checked his rifle there was no round in the chamber. Apparently, he had been so coked up that he had chambered the rifle before placing a full .30 round clip in it. Jim Cernich, Mike Imperial and I had made entry into the room while Jack Schliep guarded the first bad guy. Afterwards I got chills as I thought about how close we came to killing someone when there was no bullet in the chamber. God seemed to always be watching over us, and sometimes over the bad guys also.

CHAPTER 20
INTERDICTION IN SOUTH FLORIDA

»»»

W orking interdiction narcotics cases in South Florida was very enjoyable. We were living the good life in those days. At times we were working with U.S. Customs out in the gulf surveilling possible drug carrying water craft. In order for us to do this we wore our Hawaiian shirts and fished and cooked out on the deck of the forty-five-foot boat which had every accommodation you could imagine. We ate well and had a good time while taking turns watching the activity of the other boats. I remember thinking to myself, "It is hard to believe I am getting paid for doing this." It would not always be fun and games, but we tried to make the most of those good times.

We utilized many undercover informants during those days, and the four of us took turns playing the bad guy on reverse stings. On one occasion I had a female informant who was loaned out to U.S. Customs on an interdiction case in South Florida. There was a group which was bringing in a large amount of marijuana to a fishing village called Goodland which is located in Collier County. My informant had infiltrated the group receiving the shipment, but she apparently was refusing to deal directly with the Customs agents, saying she had been burned by them on a previous occasion. I was at home asleep one night when I received a phone call from the AIC (Agent in Charge) of Customs in South Florida. He said they needed immediate help as the drugs were coming in by shrimp boat, but they did not know when or where. After receiving approval from higher ups, I called our pilot, Mike Richie, who met me at the Inverness Airport, and we took off for South Florida in a single engine fixed wing plane. It was dark, and Mike had to fly by his instruments. We landed on Marco Island and proceeded to a U.S. Forestry camp site where we slept, and I waited for the informant to contact me. The next morning, I debriefed with the Customs agents, and was immediately struck by the lack of experience that all but one had. Three of them had only recently made lateral transfers from other non-law enforcement Federal Agencies. I made recommendations about where the drugs might be off loaded based on my informant's information, but this was met with indifference. The night the drugs were being unloaded under the Goodland Bridge, all of the Customs Agents decided to go to a party. Mike and I decided after a while that we could not work with these guys, so we went back to the plane and left.

The night after I got home, I received another call from the AIC. He wanted to know why we left and told me they really needed my help if I would come back. I decided I would, but I was in no great hurry to get there. The next morning, I got into the blue customized corvette we had previously seized in a drug deal and drove back to Collier County. The drugs had already been off-loaded right under the noses of the agents and were stored in a farm house. The bad guys were also at the house. Based on an affidavit supported by the informant we were able to affect a search warrant which was served by the agents. Several bad guys were arrested, and the catch of drugs was seized. I made sure they paid my informant who initially had to be arrested with the bad guys in order to remove suspicion from her. Customs looked good, and they got positive press on the case. I returned to Citrus County. This was the only negative experience I ever had with U.S. Customs. All others were extremely positive.

CHAPTER 21
INTERDICTION, PLANES, AND DRUGS

»»»

T he phone rang as I was sleeping soundly in my bed
at home. As was our normal routine, Susan would
pick up the phone and hand it to me while continuing
to sleep. The voice on the other end was Sgt. Jim
Beebe. He related that while on routine patrol near the
Inverness airport, his vehicle was stopped by two men
in camos who identified themselves as C.I.A. operatives. They showed him identification which appeared
to be legitimate and told him they were conducting an
operation in the area, and they ordered him to clear
the area and leave. Intuitively, Jim related later that
the whole thing seemed very suspicious. Jim left the
area and immediately called Capt. Jimmy Hill. Capt.
Hill told him to call me and my men out and get us
involved. I called the guys and we met Sgt. Beebe at
the Inverness airport. When we arrived, we cleared
the area and found no one. We went to the exact area
where Sgt. Beebe was confronted which was right in
front of one of the hangers. We were able to identify
who the owner of the hanger and noticed it had a new

pad-lock on the door. We called the owner out and when he arrived, we asked him to open the lock. He tried but his key would not work in the lock. We got some bolt cutters, and with the owner's permission, we cut off the lock.

After opening the hanger, we discovered his single engine Cessna had been partially repainted and the N numbers had been changed. We decided to spread out and search the area within about a hundred yards of our location. In a tall grassy area about fifty yards from the hanger, we discovered a military duffel bag. We searched the duffel bag and were shocked at the contents we found. Inside the bag there were multiple legitimate looking identifications from: The Central Intelligence Agency, The Federal Bureau of Investigation, and many others. Another interesting thing we found was a car title. This title proved to be very crucial to this case. We now had a description and color of a vehicle. We also found a tag registration. We alerted all of our patrol units, and the four of us set up on the airport. We knew they had not finished their business, and they would be back. Several hours later Eddie Bevill driving one of our marked units spotted the vehicle making its way back into Inverness. I told him to wait for back-up and then take them down. They accomplished this, and when we arrived, they had two individuals in camos on the ground….face down. We cuffed them, advised them of their rights, and transported them to the Sheriff's Department.

The leader was a diminutive man whom I will refer to as Mitch. We began to debrief Mitch and he cooperated willingly. We soon discovered there were three of them. They had been living in the Gainesville, Florida area, and they were very well connected. Mitch was especially connected since he was the leader of the group. His associate, who I will call Freddy, was not cooperating initially, but appeared to be a minor player who was just along for the ride. Mitch, on the other hand, was not only well connected, but was an electronics genius, an accomplished pilot, and could make up identifications which only an expert could determine whether or not they were valid.

During this time the F.B.I. (Federal Bureau of Investigation) had been charged by the President to share in working Drug cases with the D.E.A. (Drug Enforcement Agency). We initially called in the F.B.I. to interview Mitch. After a short amount of time, the Agent came out of the room and told us he didn't feel Mitch could do anything for them. I was astonished at this remark. We contacted Manny Pandakis, D.E.A. Special Agent out of Tampa, Florida, and he immediately came to the office to interview Mitch. After talking for over two hours, Manny came out and proclaimed, "We want him." The D.E.A. took Mitch. Freddy stayed in jail, and Mike Imperial, Jim Cernich, John Hemmer,

Jim Beebe and I left for Gainesville to arrest the third member of the group. We were all wearing camos with our guns and badges on the outside.

Upon our arrival in Gainesville we hooked up with the Gainesville Police Department, and with the help of one of their investigators we were able to secure a search warrant through a Judge in that area. The five of us, along with the Gainesville investigator, went to the residence where the bad guys had been living. It was a white, cinder block garage apartment with the living quarters upstairs. Mitch had warned us that his partner would be armed, and asked us to try not to shoot him. We climbed the stairwell outside the apartment with guns drawn. Just as we reached the top of the stairs, we heard a gunshot from within. We all pancaked against the side of the building, believing the man inside was shooting at us. We waited several moments and then kicked the door in. We did not have to shoot the man inside. He had already accomplished that. He was lying the way he had fallen, on a cot on the living room floor, with the gun still in his hand. After removing the gun from his hand, I sat down on the cot next to him and watched the life drain from his body as his eyes began to turn pale. I had watched others die in the past, but this one seemed to be so unnecessary. "Why?" I asked rhetorically, because I knew he could not respond. We surmised that when his two friends had not returned, he must have known something had gone wrong. When he saw armed men with guns out-side his apartment, he may have thought we were bad guys coming after him and he feared being tortured. Whatever the case was, he was now dead, and no one but God would ever know what He was thinking in those moments before He ended his life.

It wasn't long before Mitch began to prove his worth to the Federal Government. He would set up many deals with Cartel members in South America, Jamaica and Mexico over the next several years. I was told by the D.E.A. that he was probably the most productive undercover informant in the whole Southeastern United States. We were able to share in some of the cases, because we had originally been the ones to flip Mitch.

On one occasion Mitch flew a vintage DC-six to Jamaica and picked up sixty-five hundred pounds of marijuana. He had landed the plane on a dirt strip, and when he tried to take off, some of the Jamaicans were climbing on board and had to be thrown off the plane while it was making its way down the runway. He said he started having engine trouble and he was forced to make an emergency landing at Guantanamo Navy Base in Cuba. He said some of the Navy mechanics came out and fixed the engine, and they were able to take off again for Tampa International Airport. As strange as it may seem, no one bothered to search the plan. This may have been an oversight, or someone in the D.E.A. may have been directing what was going on.

Upon arrival at Tampa International, the dope was off loaded into a warehouse not too far from the airport. Three sets of buyers had been previously arranged. They were coming in from New Orleans, New York and Louisville, Kentucky. They would be driving Winnebagos and some bad guys along with one undercover would load them up. The plan was to allow the first two groups to get out on Dale Mabry Highway and we would take them down there. This was done so the next groups would not see anything upon their arrival. The last group would be taken down inside the warehouse. I remember how my heart was pounding when we took down the first group. We surrounded the Winnebago and stopped it in the middle of the highway. It was dark and another undercover and I jumped up on the front of the vehicle, pointing our guns at the driver and ordering him to get his hands in the air. We did the same with the second group. Now it was time to take down the third group inside the warehouse.

As we huddled outside the warehouse in a wooded area, the Special Agent in Charge gave us instructions about the take down. He said he had an undercover inside, and he didn't want any of us shooting him. He described him as a black male who would be wearing a red plaid shirt. When we got the word, we rushed in to the warehouse exclaiming, "Police," and telling everyone to get their hands in the air. As we did this I looked around and saw three black men all wearing red plaid shirts. I grabbed the first one I got to and threw him up against the vehicle. I had my gun to the back of his head. The agent in charge walked in, and as he walked past me, he tapped me on the shoulder and said, "He's mine." I asked the undercover why he had not said something and he said he wasn't going to say anything with a gun held to the back of his head. These were the types of cases we worked during that time. We were living on the edge and enjoying every minute of it. It seemed to be one adventure after another. I always prayed for God's protection and guidance, but I don't believe I realized at the time…..just how much He was protecting us. I now know, He had dispatched angels to watch over us.

CHAPTER 22
THE REVERSE STING

»»»

Mike Imperial had made arrangements With U.S. Customs for us to pick up approximately five hundred pounds of marijuana to be used in reverse stings. This was dope which had been seized by customs agents as it was being smuggled into this country through various methods. We drove down to South Florida in a pick-up truck with a camper shell on the back which had clear glass windows around the sides. We arrived at a secret warehouse that was guarded very carefully by armed guards. Inside the warehouse I was taken back by the sheer volume of dope I saw. Tons of marijuana stacked on pallets, sometimes four or five pallets high. This place, I thought to myself, would be a drug dealer's fantasy. We were able to pick out a high grade of sinsemilla, (a high grade of marijuana) that we felt would be very attractive to dealers in Citrus County. After loading the bales on the back of the truck, (ten bales of approximately fifty pounds each) we headed out for Citrus County.

A funny thing happened along the way. We got lost and ended up in downtown Liberty City. Now Liberty City is a section of Miami which was infested with gang activity, and most cops didn't venture there during night time hours. We pulled up to a red light and there was a gang of young men standing on the corner. Picture two white men with a pick-up loaded down with marijuana in Liberty City in broad daylight. The young men were pointing at the truck and saying things to each other which we could only imagine. We readied our weapons for what might take place next, but nothing happened. We figured later that they surmised the situation was so outrageous to them that it must be a set-up. Two white men would never drive a pick-up truck loaded with dope, into their neighborhood and in broad daylight if it wasn't. God was once again watching over us, even if we didn't realize it at the time.

On another occasion, we had an informant set up a buy of fifty pounds of dope for thirty-five thousand dollars in cash money. The informant and I were to meet up with the two bad guys at a convenience store and then follow them to an undisclosed location in the forest. I was wearing a bug which had a mic taped to my chest. When we arrived, introductions were made. I was using my undercover name of Bud Baxley and the two bad guys I will refer to as Sonny and his partner, Tim. We had a predetermined code that I would say when the deal was done letting my men know it was time to move in and make the arrests.

Upon arriving at the place in the forest, we excited our vehicles and exchanged limited small talk. Suddenly Sonny, who was quite an imposing figure at six foot four and about two hundred and sixty pounds, raised his shirt showing a 357 six- inch revolver in his belt, and exclaimed, "O.K, before we get started you can search me and I am going to search you, to make sure nobody is wearing a wire." I knew I had to think fast so I said, "No, you sound like you may be a cop to me, and you're not putting your hands on me; and, if you're wondering if I have a gun, well I do." I knew a common trait among those in the drug culture was paranoia. The more paranoid you act, the more believable you are. This seemed to satisfy Sonny and he said, "O.K, let's forget it and just do the deal." We got the dope out of our vehicle and I asked about the money. Sonny told me it was over behind a palmetto bush under a palmetto leaf. As I started to walk toward the bush, I saw Sonny putting his hand on his gun. I turned toward him putting my hand on my gun and backed up toward the bush. It suddenly occurred to me that this might all be a set-up, and they intended to kill us, and take the dope and the money. Very slowly I bent down while keeping my eyes on Sonny. I retrieved the clear plastic bag with the money inside and then walked back toward the other three men. I continued to keep my hand on my gun the entire time.

Sonny said, "Aren't you going to count it?" "No," I said, "If it's not right, I will find you." Not willing to give up, Sonny said, if it was alright, his Buddy would take the dope, and he would get us to drop him off down the road. I knew if we allowed him to get in the back seat, he was going to take us out and take back the money. I refused and told him the deal was over, and they needed to just take the dope and leave. I had given the code words twice, but no one moved in. We parted ways with Sonny and Tim leaving. I got on a portable radio and inquired where everyone was. The answer I got was, they didn't have any idea where we were. The battery in the bug had gone dead and they had no idea where we were! When my informant heard this, he got ill and started throwing up. I had been very brave, thinking my men were watching me and ready to move in at any time. It's probably best that I didn't know. During the time we were closing the deal, Tim kept saying I looked familiar to him and that he thought he might know me. I told him no, and just try to play off his comments. When we took Tim down at a roadblock, I walked up to Tim, and he called me by my right name. He said he kept thinking that he knew who I was; and after they left the meeting, he remembered. God was once again watching over me.

I had an informant inside of Sonny's family. I will just call this person Q. I met with Q every now and then to find out what Sonny was doing. Sonny had not yet gone to trial, and he knew I would be the State's primary witness against him. During one of my late-night meetings with Q, I was informed that Sonny had many friends in organized crime in the Tampa area. Q said Sonny had taken out a contract on me, and I needed to be very careful. I wasn't sure how credible this information was, but I would soon find out.

One day soon after, my daughter, Bridget, alerted me that a blue pick-up truck was driving slowly by our house. We lived on a dead-end street with not many houses. When a vehicle which I didn't know came by, I always took note of it. The truck went to the end of the street and turned around and came back and slowed down in front of my house. I recognized the driver as being Tim. I knew he had been sent by Sonny to find out where I lived. I became extremely furious. Now they were not just messing with me. They were endangering my wife and children also.

I realized this was an extreme situation that called for an extreme solution. I got ready and went to the other side of the county to where Tim lived in a sin-gle-wide mobile home. I will premise this next state-ment by saying that I never intended to carry out this threat, but I had to convince Tim that I would. I knocked on the door, and when he opened it, I stepped in with my gun drawn and stuck it in his face. I backed him inside and up against the refrigerator. I asked him where his family was and he told me he was home alone. I could tell that he was scared, and I knew I had to make him believe what I was about to say. I asked him what he was doing over at my house, and he replied that Sonny had sent him to verify where I lived. I told him I had a message for him and one for Sonny. You tell Sonny that if one of my children so much as stubbed their toe coming home from school, I would hold both of them responsible. I told him if they sent someone to my house, they better not miss. I said that they had no idea what I was capable of doing. I told him I would come back over there and kill his whole family while he watched, and then kill him last. I told him that next I would go to Sonny's house and kill his whole family before killing him. I told him to deliver the message to Sonny. I left hoping that I had been believable. Soon after I was contacted by Q. Q said they did not know what I had done, but the contract had been lifted. Sonny and Tim were both convicted and served time.

CHAPTER 23
HUMOROUS DRUG CASES

>>»>

While working narcotics was very serious business, sometimes funny things occurred which we would laugh about and talk about in years to come. On one occasion, Mike Imperial and I were working an informant who had probably done a few too many drugs. We had him set up to make a controlled buy from a known drug dealer, and we had wired him with an undercover listening device. Mike explained to him that when he was walking toward the drug dealer's house, he was to say his own name, the name of the dealer he was making the buy from and the date and time. As he was walking toward the residence, he did everything we had requested, but when he got to the date he said, "Today is July 32." After he completed the buy, we asked him why he said July 32. In a very matter of fact way, he replied that it must be because the previous day was July 31. His reasoning almost made sense, almost!

In another case we were doing surveillance on a known drug dealer's residence, and had watched several people go to the residence, make buys, and leave. The suspect was doing a lot of business, but we did not have an informant who could get inside to make a buy for us… thereby giving us probable cause for a search warrant. Finally, we came up with a plan. The suspect, who I will refer to as John, was at home along with his brother. The brother was charged with greeting prospective buyers at the door and escorting them inside to John where the deals were made. We decided to just go and knock on the front door and ask for John and see what happened. We went to the front door and knocked, and when the brother came to the door, we asked for John. The brother invited us in, and told us John was in the back room. As we walked down the hallway the door to the room was open, and John was weighing up cocaine in plain view. We placed him under arrest, and he started yelling accusations that we had entered without a search warrant. We explained to him that we didn't need a warrant since his brother had invited us in. He cursed his brother yelling, "What were you thinking?" Sometimes the simplest plans worked out well.

All of our duties didn't always include narcotics. On one occasion, we were contacted by one of our informants, who said a prominent Crystal River business man was looking for a hit man to take out a Judge, a prosecutor and the Sheriff. We brought up an undercover deputy from Hernando County and arranged an introduction. I will just call the businessman Bob. We arranged for Bob to meet with our undercover (UC) in the parking lot of a shopping Center. UC had been wired with a listening device, and we were parked about 100 feet from Bob's vehicle. UC drove up in his vehicle and got into Bob's vehicle, and after exchanging introductions, UC got right to the point. He asked Bob specifically who he wanted taken out. He had Bob to describe the way they were to be killed, and eventually they began to discuss money. An agreement was made on the amount of money; however, Bob was having trouble coming up with any money over the next several days, and so we made the decision to go ahead and arrest Bob on a warrant for, "Conspiracy to Commit Murder." Since no money ever exchanged hands, the State was forced to accept a plea to a lesser charge. Bob never served any time, I don't believe. I learned early on that our job was to investigate, put bad guys in jail, and testify in court. All else was the responsibility of the State Attorney and the court system. I would depend on God to judge the ones who got away.

CHAPTER 24
NOTHING PERSONAL

»»»

O n one occasion I was in a deposition over a drug case. The lawyer was a very high-priced attorney out of Miami who specialized in drug cases. He deposed me for over two hours. When the depositions were over, he and I went out to lunch. This gave me an opportunity to ask him a few questions. He told me all of his clients had to come up with a ten-thousand-dollar retainer before he would even talk to them. Keep in mind that in those days, this was more than a half year salary for me. He said he approached all cases the same way. He said law enforcement always makes mistakes, and it was his job to find and over embellish those mistakes in court. In this case he ended up cutting a deal and pleading his client guilty. This made me feel like we had made a pretty good case. I learned that you could not take it personally. Everyone had a job to do… including the defense attorneys.

CHAPTER 25
A NEW ADVENTURE

»»»

D ue to the threats which had been made against my life, Sheriff Dean felt it was necessary to take me out of narcotics and place me back in patrol for a period of time. He had a lot of wisdom about these things and looking back, I know this was the right thing to do. I became a shift supervisor and did this for about a year. Corporal Jack Roberts was assigned to work with me and together we supervised a shift of deputies covering Citrus County.

There were always exciting things taking place during this time. On one occasion, a prisoner had escaped custody from one of our investigators. When I responded to the area near Homosassa Springs, I began to drive around the area looking for anything that might seem out of sorts. As I drove past a vacated double-wide mobile home, I noticed something strange. The residence was empty, the windows were open but there was a window air-conditioner running full blast. I got out of my cruiser and decided to investigate. I looked through the front windows and verified that the residence was empty. This created a sense of dejavue. Had I not been in this situation once before. I began to tremble as I recalled what had happened previously. I knew, just as I had done in the previous situation, it was necessary for me to press forward and do what needed to be done. After walking up on the front porch I tried the front door and found it to be unlocked. Drawing my pistol, I yelled out, "Sheriff's Department. Come out with your hands up." With my gun in hand, I began to search the premises. My heart was beating rapidly as I cleared the rooms, one by one. Working my way from one room to the other I encountered one empty room after the other. When I entered the master bedroom, I quickly went to the clothes closet and slid the door aside. Sticking my head inside, I looked to the left first and saw nothing. When I looked to the right I was staring at a man's mid-section. Jumping back, I told him. "Come out with your hands where I can see them." He complied initially, but I saw something in his eyes that told me he once again had rabbit fever and was about to make a break for it. Immediately, I took him to the floor and handcuffed him. After taking him to my car and securing him in the back, I notified deputy Woody Lucius who took him and booked him into the county jail. Only then, when I was alone did I begin to calm myself about what had just occurred.

People who have never experienced P.T.S.D., would never understand the emotional rollercoaster it can create in a situation like that. I thanked God for protecting me once again. I continued to press forward, with God's help, to do the job before me. After a year had gone by, I was on vacation in Alabama when I received a call from Sheriff Dean. He told me, upon my return, he was placing me in charge of General Investigation. I would once again answer to Terry Lacasse who had been promoted to Captain over the Criminal Investigation Division. This seemed like a natural fit for me, and I enjoyed the next four years in that capacity. There were many interesting cases we worked during those days. This included Serial murderer, Eileen Wournos. I, along with my men, were called out to work the murder of David Spears who was found in a rural wooded area of our county. I did not have direct involvement in her arrest and prosecution, but several of our investigators participated in her arrest. She later received the death penalty and was executed by the State of Florida.

CHAPTER 26
THE OGLES' CASE

»»»

One of the most intriguing cases I ever worked was the kidnapping and Murder of Gloria Ogles. Mrs. Ogles, along with her husband Leroy, owned and operated a very successful roofing business in Crystal River, Florida. One day, while at work; her daughter, Julie, left the business to go and pick up lunch for her and her mother. When Julie returned, she discovered that her mother was missing. Not being able to locate her mother, and seeing her mother's car was still parked outside, Julie called 911 to report her mother's disappearance. After the initial responders arrived and determined there may be foul play, I and a team of investigators were called.

When we arrived, we began to piece together what may have occurred. There was some rope lying on the floor next to Mrs. Ogles' chair. We surmised that a piece may have been used to tie her up and abduct her from the scene. Whoever did this could not have brought her out through the front of the business, because it fronted a very busy highway, and they would have been seen. We used a search dog and began to follow a trail which led through the warehouse and down an isolated, gravel road which ran behind the business. At a certain location, about one hundred yards from the business, the trail stopped. We found a pullover camo, wool hat in the ditch at this location. Holes had been cut in the hat for eyes. We determined that this was used as a mask. We now felt Mrs. Ogles had, in fact, been abducted; but the reason why was a mystery. We, along with the family, waited to see if there were any calls or letters demanding a ransom. However, nothing ever came. The phones at the home and business were tapped, but.... no calls. There were no witnesses and no suspects. We were able to retrieve a few blond hairs from the wool hat but we found no fingerprints at the scene. I knew this would be a very difficult case to solve. At the direction of Sheriff Dean, Jerry Thompson and I worked this case to conclusion.

After several weeks, we had exhausted every lead that we had; but still had nothing. The family was becoming very impatient with the progress we were making. They had a right to be upset. After all, this was their wife and mother, and this was a large family.

We got our first break when we discovered that Mrs. Ogles' debit card was used at an ATM machine in the mall in Ocala, Florida. After checking bank records, we noticed another transaction was made at the same ATM machine immediately after Mrs. Ogle's card was used.

We had previously advised the family to allow the continued use of her card, as this might provide a valuable clue. With the bank's assistance, we were able to learn the name and a contact number for the lady who had used the ATM immediately after Mrs. Ogles' card was used. Jerry Thompson and I interviewed her and we found out the following information. She said she did remember using the ATM on that date, and she recalled seeing the young man in front of her. The lady was a beautician by trade, and she paid close attention to the man's hair and looks. She further stated that the young man kept looking at a young woman with long blond hair standing in the doorway of a nearby shop with a worried look on her face. The young man retrieved some cash and left with the young woman.

We asked the woman if she could remember the young man well enough to describe him to a forensic artist who could draw a picture of the suspect based on the description. She said she would try to do this. We had the woman accompany us back to the Sheriff's Department in Inverness, and we made contact with Linda Galener, a forensic artist in Tallahassee. We made arrangements for Mike Ritchie, a pilot in our department, to fly to Tallahassee, pick up Linda Galener, and bring her back to Inverness. Once there, the woman began to describe the suspect to Linda, and a composite drawing was accomplished. We now had a composite drawing of a suspect, and that picture was circulated to law enforcement agencies across the state.

It was along this time, while hunting, that two hunters were in the Citrus Springs area in the north end of the county when they discovered a body. The body was lying in a remote, wooded area about twenty-five feet off of the roadway. We responded to the scene and made a temporary identification of the body. It was Mrs. Ogles. Now came the arduous task of notifying the family. This was one of the most difficult things I had to accomplish during my entire career in law enforcement, and it never became easy for me to notify a family member of a deceased loved one.

Dave Strickland and his team of evidence technicians were called to the scene, and the long and tedious task of processing the crime scene began. Adjacent to the crime scene and next to the road was a dried up, sandy bottomed storm water retention pond. In the sandy bottom, we discovered what appeared to be shoe prints in the sand which led to a five-foot culvert pipe which ran under the road and ended on the other side in a squared concrete storm drain. Dave Strickland led the way as the three of us crawled and waddled through the pipe going under the road. Dave discovered blood on the floor of the pipe in several locations before reaching the other end. At the end we discovered several things. Imbedded in the back wall we found implanted in the concrete, two eye bolts. In a smaller pipe, which ran parallel to the road, we discovered more blood and a shell casing which appeared to come from a .25 cal. weapon. We began to piece together what had occurred at this location. Apparently, the suspect had kidnapped her and brought her to this location and had her cuffed or tied her to the eye bolts. At some point, he had shot her in the head, but not before retrieving her ATM card and getting her to give up her password. It had been published in the paper that the company had received a large sum of money, and the suspect probably thought he could get more with the ATM card. What he did not realize was that only a limited amount of money could be withdrawn at one time.

There appeared to be drag marks leading from the pipe up to the roadway, and it was there that we discovered skid marks and tire tracks. We also discovered two small two-inch circular pieces of camo wool which we later determined had been cut from the camo wool cap that was found near the roofing business. All of these pieces of evidence proved to be valuable as we pieced together what had occurred. Apparently, after being shot, Ms. Ogles crawled up to the roadway, where she was run over by a car. However, she still managed to drag herself into the woods, where she later died. The bullet wound to the head, the fractured hyoid bone in her throat and being run over with a car, and yet this brave, resilient woman still fought to stay alive. She was a very remarkable woman.

After observing photographs, charts, and the autopsy report provided by Doctor Schultz, the Chief Medical Examiner; Jerry Thompson and I traveled to Gainesville to meet with Dr. William Maples. Everyone had heard of Doctor Maples. Dr. Maples was considered one of the world's foremost authorities in the area of forensic anthropology. He was able to determine, after studying the width of the tire tread and the marks the tires left on Mrs. Ogles' body, how her own fist had rotated across her throat, as the tire rolled over her, causing the fracture to her hyoid bone, and thus leading to her death. All of this important information would be critical during the trial…..if and when we ever arrested a suspect.

The investigation of this case became an obsession for Jerry and myself. We worked many tireless hours for weeks, but every lead proved to be a dead end. Everyone else in the department including detectives and patrolmen spent untold numbers of hours interviewing suspects and talking to people, but nothing turned up. I decided that this case would never be solved without the help of God. I knew if I prayed, and if others prayed, God would direct me in what I must do. I knew I must be willing to listen to what He was telling me and respond accordingly.

One day, while working, I felt impressed that I needed to get alone with God, pray, and listen for direction. This was something I did many times during my career, and it would often yield positive results. I told Jerry I was going out on my own that day, and I got in my car and started driving around in the Crystal River area. While driving I began to pray and seek God for answers. As I was driving around, I felt impressed to stop in front of a small, concrete block house. God was telling me to go to the front door and talk to the people there. I wanted to be obedient, but I had no idea what I would say, or if they may think me to be an idiot. I went up to the front door, knocked, and a little old lady, who appeared to be in her eighties, came to the door and greeted me with, "Hello, may I help you?" Embarrassed and not knowing exactly what to say, I finally identified myself and told her I was investigating the abduction and murder of Gloria Ogles. I went on to tell her that I had felt God impressing me to stop at this house, and that the reason would become apparent at some point. She invited me into her house, and as she did so, she told me her husband was a retired Baptist preacher. She told me they had become very interested in the case and had agreed in prayer many times that God would help someone solve the case.

After meeting her husband and talking briefly to the two of them, I asked if they would hold hands with me and pray over me that God would help me to solve the case. After we prayed, I left their house…not having any idea what had been accomplished. Little did I know God was already putting things in motion that would resolve everything very quickly.

That night, I was going to bed when I received a phone call from one of the investigators in the department. It was Marvin Padgett. Marvin began to relate to me the following story. He said he had been working a burglary case, and he had a suspect in custody. He said he and a couple of other investigators were getting ready to execute a search warrant on a residence in the Crystal River area. He told me they believed there was stolen property located in the residence and that they hoped to retrieve the property and possibly a gun. It was already after dark, and we usually didn't serve search warrants after dark. He asked if I would like to go along with them on the search warrant.

There were several things which made this unusual. First of all, we hardly ever served search warrants at night, and secondly, I usually did not go on a search warrant on a case unless I was directly involved. For some strange reason, I felt compelled to go on this one. I agreed to go, got dressed, and drove down to the sheriffs' operations building. Upon my arrival, I noticed there was a young man sitting in a chair next to Marvin's desk. Something about him caught my eye, and I remembered thinking to myself that the man looked a lot like the picture Linda Galener had drawn. It had been several months since the kidnapping and murder of Gloria Ogles, and I hoped I wasn't just grasping at straws. I told Marvin I would like to speak with the man before we left to execute the search warrant. I escorted him into my office, we sat down, and I began to question him about the Ogles case. He told me he had heard about the case, but he had no knowledge of the case or the people involved. Marvin, John Plevell and I then left with the suspect and went to Crystal River where we executed the search warrant at his home, which was also the home of his father. He was only 17 years old, but he had already celebrated a pretty extensive, criminal past. After returning to the sheriffs' department in Inverness, I decided I would question the man a little more thoroughly about the Ogles case. Once again, I took him into my office and asked him a very leading question. I asked him where he was on the Wednesday that Mrs. Ogles was kidnapped. Without hesitation, he told me he was at home that day with his girlfriend, and they were working on his truck. Without realizing it, he had given me the first crucial information that led me to believe that he was, in fact, involved in the case.

It had been several months since Mrs. Ogles' abduction, and I knew that anyone who would immediately know where they were on a particular Wednesday from several months before, would have to have a reason to remember that particular day. He continued to stress he had no knowledge of the case. At the time Marvin and John had arrested him on the burglary case, he had his girlfriend with him; and she was incarcerated in the women's section of the jail across the street. Once again, I felt impressed and compelled to go over and question her. It was pretty late at night, and all of the prisoners had gone to sleep. I told the corrections officers to go upstairs and wake her and bring her down because I needed to interrogate her. Once I was in a room with her and had advised her of her constitutional rights, I began to question her about the Ogles' case. Initially she denied any knowledge about the case, and it was at this point that I decided to utilize some investigative deception. I led her to believe that we had eyewitnesses who would testify that she and her boyfriend were in the mall in Ocala, Florida, using Mrs. Ogles' debit card to withdraw money from a walk-up ATM machine. It was, at this point, that she made a statement which would break this case wide open. She admitted that she was with him when he withdrew money from the ATM machine, but she did not know, at that point, that he had murdered Mrs. Ogles. I took a taped confession from her, called Jerry Thompson, and told him what was going on. Jerry met me at the sheriffs' department, and we began to plan our strategy about interviewing the suspect.

By the time we got our ducks in a row, the suspect had been transferred to Ocala, Florida, where there was a lockup for both juveniles and youthful offenders. Jerry and I went to Ocala and briefed Brad King, who was an assistant state attorney, about the case. We had the suspect brought to an interview room where we once again informed him of his rights and recorded an interview with him. I told him his girlfriend had already confessed, and we were going to charge both of them with kidnapping and murder. He said if we would leave his girlfriend out of it, he would give us a full confession. For the next hour Jerry and I interrogated him, and he provided a detailed confession about what happened. It seems that he had been a previous employee of the roofing company and was aware of the layout of the offices and warehouse. He further stated he had heard about the company receiving a large amount of money in a lawsuit, and he thought he could access this money using Mrs. Ogles' ATM card.

All the hard work we had invested in this case, over several months, had finally come to fruition. I knew that God had directed me in what had been accomplished, and that it was only through him that we were able to solve this case. I recounted in my mind the previous day's activities when God had told me to stop at the little house in Crystal River and talk to the couple there. While I did not understand the significance or the reason for what I was doing, God was teaching me obedience. I know now that sometimes we do not understand the immediate reason for things which God tells us to do, but He has a very intricate plan for our lives, and if we are obedient, we will reap the rewards of our obedience at some point.

During the time we were investigating this case, we consulted with two special agents from F.D.L.E. (Florida Department of Law Enforcement.) One of those agents, Dale Hinman, who was a criminal profiler, would...after her retirement, have her own television show called *Body of Evidence*. She contacted me years later, while I was living in Alabama, and asked if I would consider coming back to Florida to film this case with her. Fifteen years after the filming, this show continues to be shown in reruns on television.

Ordinarily, my job would have been accomplished with this case, but there were some important details which had to be cleared up. After the autopsy, the medical examiner had stated that Mrs. Ogles had been dead approximately a month at the time of the autopsy, but according to the defendant it was only about two weeks. We knew this discrepancy might be a problem when we went to trial. Jerry Thompson made the arrangements, and the two of us made a trip to Knoxville, Tennessee, to meet with Dr. William Bass. Dr. Bass was considered the world's foremost authority on the decomposition of bodies. We carried with us; still photographs, weather charts, insect infestation documentation, and the autopsy report. I knew we were hoping for him to come back with a two-week time period. I asked Dr. Bass before leaving if he could look at our evidence briefly and give me a preliminary guess as to how long she had been deceased. He carefully looked at the evidence we had given him for about five minutes and then proclaimed, "I think about fourteen days." I was totally blown away by his statement. It was exactly correct. I knew at that moment I was witnessing the best there was.

I have deliberately omitted the name of the suspect in this case, due to his age at the time of occurrence. The trial did not take place. The defense felt the evidence against him was so overwhelming that he persuaded him to plead guilty, and serve two consecutive life sentences for kidnapping and murder. Some family members were not happy with this agreement, but if he had received the death penalty, and the sentence was later reduced to life, he would have gotten out much sooner.

During the four years I was in charge of General Investigation, I worked and was involved in many interesting cases where God showed up in a special way, and used me, a most unlikely person, to solve those cases. I do not underestimate God's help, or the great work that others in the Criminal Investigations Department provided which helped to solve many of these cases. Jerry Thompson, John Plevel, Marvin

Padgett, Bob Horton, Woody Lucius, Jack Schliep and Larry Burkhalter all worked with me, side by side to solve many major crimes during those years. We were supported by an excellent team of evidence technicians, Dave Strickland, Tim Parker and Diana Crowder. Henry Wilkins provided supervision for a while during that time. Terry Lacasse was the Captain over CID, and he did a great job of supervising the unit and giving us the freedom to work unencumbered and without micro-management.

CHAPTER 27
MURDER FOR HIRE

»»»

It was late one night, and Susan and I were asleep in bed when the phone rang. Susan was so accustomed to this occurring that she reached for the phone, which was on the side table on her side of the bed, and handed it over to me with one swift calculated move and then went back to sleep. When I answered, it was Wayne Burns, a patrol supervisor on the night shift, and he started out by saying. "We have a house down here near Floral City, and there are dead bodies everywhere; and there may be a bad guy still inside of the house." Not being fully awake yet, I asked him to repeat what he had just said. I told him to surround the house until I was able to assemble some of the guys, and we would get there as soon as possible.

On the way to Floral City I remember thinking to myself, how normal things were for most people in the area. Families had gone to bed that night, just as they would on most nights, never suspecting something so heinous and terrible had occurred in their community. It was what appeared to be a normal night, but this night was anything but normal. A mass murder had occurred in this sleepy little community, and four people had lost their lives. After arriving, I decided to call for a search dog, and we assembled a search team to enter the house and check for bad guys. It seems that the responding deputies had heard a noise inside the house, which we later determined to be a death rattle from one of the deceased. The girlfriend of one of the victims had arrived home after being at the hospital with her mother, and upon entering the house in the dark, because the power had been cut off; she stumbled over two bodies and hurriedly left the house. The search team, including myself, entered the house with protective gear, guns drawn, and flashlights in hand. We discovered a total of four bodies in different locations which had died from various methods, but all were deceased. The only survivor was the lady who lived there but was not home at the time of the murders. After discovering the dead consisted of; her boyfriend, a worker who had been hired by the boyfriend, the next-door neighbor and an employee of the next-door neighbor; a pattern started to reveal itself...... especially after the lady told us she was supposed to have been at home. She had to leave suddenly to take her sick mother to the emergency room and found everyone dead upon her return. I suspicioned that she might have also been a target, and after conferring with Captain Lacasse, I requested to place the lady in a safe house. This was a place, known only to us, where she could hide until we had a chance to figure things out and ensure her protection.

Without our knowing it at the time, this proved to be a very valuable strategy. We had previously secured the scene, and as daylight arrived, David Strickland and his team of evidence technicians began to process the crime scene. This proved to be a very difficult task for them, but we felt like they were the best evidence people around, and this proved to be true many times over the years.

Without getting in to all of the investigation which followed, I will just attempt to summarize what had taken place. Apparently, the lady, who I will refer to as Jane, was going through a nasty divorce with her ex-husband who lived about a hundred miles to the north. He had been ordered to pay her a very large settlement by the court, and decided he would rather hire someone to kill her, and keep the money. It was extremely strange that he recruited his two adult sons to carry out the murder against their mother. A man who was employed at a hospital in Gainesville, Florida, was eventually selected by the sons, and was under contract to kill their mother. Their father never had any direct contact with the killer; and therefore, was able to keep himself out of the loop.

The killer was an obvious amateur and had never done anything like this before. I believe he had visions of grandeur and envisioned himself as a hitman like those he had seen in the movies. Several days prior to the murders, the hitman, who I will refer to as Sam, stopped at Jane's house while giving pretense of looking for some unknown person and befriended Jane, her boyfriend and a handyman, who the boyfriend had hired. Jane's boyfriend and the handyman had been remodeling the house in which she and her boyfriend had been living. Sam made one more trip to the residence and developed a plan as to when he would carry out the murder, what his escape route would be, and where he would leave his vehicle. On the day of the planned assassination, three things occurred which had not been according to Sam's plan. First, Jane received a call that her mother, who lived nearby, had become very sick; and Jane had to carry her to the emergency room in Inverness, Florida. Secondly, as Jane was leaving for the hospital after picking up her mother, she spotted Sam's vehicle parked beside the highway about fifty yards from her residence. She remembered his vehicle from the two previous trips to see them, and wondered what it was doing there. Thirdly, the boyfriend had also left to go to Inverness to rent a sander to be used in refinishing the hardwood floors. When Sam arrived, the only person there was the handyman. Sam slipped up behind the handyman and shot him in the back of the head using a pistol with a homemade silencer. The silencer jammed, and he finished him off by using a sheetrock axe. Sam then waited for Jane to return. A neighbor, who lived next door, had heard the gunshot and decided to come over and investigate. Upon entering the house, he was attacked by Sam, and was also killed with the same sheetrock axe. Sam waited…..but still no Jane. A man who worked for the neighbor became worried when his boss had not returned, so he decided to go find out what had happened to him. Sam attacked him and killed him with the sheetrock axe also. Jane, the intended victim, was nowhere to be found. Three men were now dead, and things were not going as planned for Sam. Next, Jane's boyfriend returned with the sander. We found out later that he put up a pretty good fight, but was also was killed with the sheetrock axe, just like the other three victims. Sam waited for hours for Jane to return, but she did not come. There were four dead men in the house, but the intended victim was still alive, and had not come home. After a while, Sam gave up and left the residence with the intended victim still alive.

When Jane arrived home after 11:00 that night, she entered the darkened house and began to trip over bodies. Scared, she ran down the road to a local tavern where she called 911. That is when we were called and got involved in the case. After a long and extensive investigation, Sam was eventually arrested in Ohio and extradited for trial. He was finally convicted of murder, and the two brothers for conspiracy to commit murder. Neither son would testify against their father nor were we able to implicate him in the case.

There were other cases, like this one, where guilty people got away with serious crimes. The criminal justice system is not perfect, but most of the time it works quite effectively.

CHAPTER 28
THE EXECUTION MURDER

»»»

hile I always prayed for guidance, when working a homicide case, God did not always provide divine intervention in every instance. There were times, however, when God would not only provide guidance, but would even speak to me about what I was supposed to do, and this would lead to the solving of cases. Christians many times fail to understand the enormous power which God has and fail to tap into his omnipotence.

An anonymous caller had reported a shooting in northwest Citrus County. The responding deputy discovered a woman dead in the bedroom of her home. She had been shot several times. After being called, I responded to the scene and along with several other detectives and evidence technicians, we began to piece together what had occurred. Deputies began to canvass the neighborhood looking for witnesses, but none were found. The woman, thirty-two-year-old Mary Lackner, had worked the midnight shift at a local convenience store. As she arrived home, there must have been an altercation in the driveway. She had

children, but they were not home at the time. We discovered her car door open and groceries on the front
seat. She must have brought the groceries home with
her from work. There were also blood spots in the
driveway. We received information from family members that there had been an ongoing domestic situation
between Mary and her ex-husband, Ronald Lackner. I
noticed a picture of Ronald Lackner in a marine uniform on the dresser. I thought to myself that this might
be useful at a later time. My assumption proved to be
true. Mary Lackner was lying on a carpet remnant next
to the bed. We found the imprint of that carpet remnant
next to the front door. She was apparently shot and
was drug to the bedroom on the carpet remnant, where
she was eventually shot again with a fatal shot through
the eye. Her top was pulled up above her breasts and
her pants were unzipped. This was probably done to
make it appear to be a sexual assault, but the autopsy
indicated a sexual assault had not happened.

After completing the crime scene work, the investigation began. We had a .22 cal. rifle, which was recovered from the corner of the living room. This was the
apparent weapon used. There were no fingerprints on
the weapon, but forensics later determined that this was
the weapon. We had no witnesses, no direct evidence to
connect anyone to the crime, and Ronald Lackner had
been living in another county. From all of the domestic
calls to the residence, and with no other suspects, we

decided to concentrate on Ronald Lackner. This seemed to be the only thing that made any sense whatsoever. There was no robbery or burglary, and there did not appear to be anyone else with a motive. A group of us traveled to the county where Ronald Lackner lived, and we set up a road-block on the road leading up to his residence. I knew, at this point, that we had no direct evidence to tie him to the crime. Thinking he was probably inside of his residence, we were trying to decide our next move when Lackner drove up to the roadblock. As was customary, we all drew our weapons until we could determine if he was armed. When I advised Ronald of his constitutional rights, I began to question him. I asked him if he had seen or talked to his ex-wife in the last several days. He said he had not. I, then, told him that Mary had been killed, and without any emotion, he simply said, "Really?" At this point I knew we were on the right track. I told him I would like for him to consent to accompany me back to the Citrus County Sheriff's Department and answer a few questions. Without hesitation he said, "Sure."

Everything seemed to be falling into place. During the ride back, I began to formulate in my mind what I would say, and how I might get him to confess. At my office there was just the two of us, since it was now after dark. I made us a cup of coffee and the two of us made small talk. He was even laughing at times, which is very strange behavior for someone who just

found out his wife had been murdered. At this point
I decided to spring it on him. Using deception as an
investigative tool, I told him I already knew he had
killed Mary. I said I had witnesses and could prove it.
I mentioned the fact that we were both former marines
and that we thought a lot alike. Without giving him
a chance to respond, I started making up a story in
which I gave him a way out. I was putting the blame
on Mary and telling him that anyone who had gone
through so much may have reacted the same way. At
this point he looked at me and said, "That's exactly
what happened." I could feel a large lump in my throat.
The fish had taken the bait.

You see, it didn't matter initially what his story was,
about the sequence of events on that day. I knew I
could work out all of the details later. What mattered
was that he confessed. I once again read him his rights,
this time on tape, and then I took his confession. One
might say the case was sewn up, but not necessarily so.
You see, sometimes during a trial, a confession may
be thrown out due to a technicality or whatever. What
was needed was one more piece of direct evidence
which could not be disputed by a judge or a jury. The
next day I went back to the crime scene looking for
that piece of evidence. Walking around inside of the
house, I prayed for divine intervention and God heard
my prayer. Going outside I once again started looking
around. I was thinking to myself, "Okay, what have I

missed? God show me something." Just as I thought this, I looked down the road, about fifty yards from my location and saw a woman watering her flowers. I knew other deputies had done a house to house search in the neighborhood interviewing the residents, but no one had seen or heard anything. What I didn't know was that the people at this residence had been gone when those interviews occurred.

Suddenly I felt God speaking to me and telling me that the woman watering her flowers had seen something. I started walking down the road, and as I got closer, I noticed the woman's husband sitting on the front steps. With boldness I approached them and said to the woman, "You saw what happened. Didn't You?" Stunned, she looked at me incredulously and didn't say a word. Suddenly her husband said, "Tell him. Tell him what you saw." She began to recount how she was outside and saw Ronald Lackner waiting with the rifle when his ex-wife arrived home. An argument ensued, and he shot her and drug her into the house. The woman stated she was terrified and that Lackner would come after her next. She went out her back door and fled to a safe location and called a friend to come and pick her up. God had supplied the extra piece of evidence that I needed to make this case. During the trial, Lackner threatened to kill me when he got out. I heard this many times over the years. However, at this writing, I am still alive, and Ronald Lackner is still in prison.

CHAPTER 29
JUSTICE FOR A RAPE VICTIM

»»»

A long this same time, there was another interesting case which took place where God gave me direction which helped me solve the case. There had been a burglary and rape which had occurred in the Homosassa Springs community. The woman, who was a single mother, awoke one night after hearing a noise inside her home. She got up and went into the living room to investigate and discovered a man going through her things. She did not yell out for fear of waking up her child. He ordered her to go back into the bedroom, and using a household product as a lubricant, he raped her. She later described him as a very diminutive, muscular white male. A standard rape kit was performed on the woman at the hospital and we were able to extract DNA from the semen which was sent to the lab. DNA was pretty new back then and there was no data base to use for comparison. We would be able to do a DNA comparison if we ever developed a suspect. We would need to extract DNA from him and send it to the lab. The woman was able to give me a pretty good description of him, but it was dark, and he was careful to not leave any fingerprints.

I drove around the Homosassa Springs community looking for anyone who might be a suspect. I went to all of the local bars and other places where I thought he might be hanging out, but it was to no avail. "Where could he be?" I thought to myself. Finally, as I did on many other occasions, I turned to my best resource. He was the one who had directed me on so many other occasions when I floundered on my own abilities. When every human resource has been tried and nothing else works, we can always turn to God, our greatest source for information and direction. I got into my car and started driving around, and as I did this I would pray. "God, I need your help, once again. Give me direction and guide my steps so I can bring this case closure and bring justice to this individual."

Homosassa Springs was a melting pot of people. Most of them had only been there for a very short time. It was a transient community where people were moving in and leaving on a regular basis. Sometimes the people living there did not even know their own neighbors, unless they had lived there for some time.

As I drove around, I now had the confidence that God would direct me and put me where I needed to be. As I slowly drove down one street, I observed something which caught my eye. Behind a double-wide mobile home there was a large deck. Sitting out on that deck, I saw a small, muscular man without a shirt with a towel around his neck. An older woman stood behind him and was cutting his hair. Thinking quickly, I stopped and got out of my car and approached the deck. I pretended to be looking for someone, whose name I quickly made up, and sat down on the deck near the people. I found out that the woman was his mother and he had recently moved in there with her. I started making random conversation, and as we talked, I placed my right hand on the deck near his chair.... as if to brace myself. When I removed my hand, I picked up some of the hair she had just cut off. The hair was sent to the lab for a DNA comparison. I had gotten his name and had asked his age while we were talking. With this information, I went back to the office and ran a criminal history using his name and a random date of birth. I knew the computer would come back with anything that was close. It also helped that he had told me he had recently moved there from Louisiana. We finally got a hit. He had served fifteen years in Angola for several felony crimes. I waited for a response from the lab, and it finally came back. It was a match. Praise God for His faithfulness and guidance.

I now had sufficient probable cause. We went to his residence and placed him under arrest. At the office, I read him his Miranda rights and proceeded to question him. I had a theory that when someone has done something that most would consider antisocial behavior, it is necessary to make their behavior seem normal in order to solicit a confession. I did this; and surprisingly, he gave me a full confession. He was convicted of the crime, and due to his previous record, he received a lengthy prison sentence.

CHAPTER 30
REFLECTIONS OF A HOMICIDE INVESTIGATOR

»»»

upervising General Investigations wasn't just about working homicides. We worked a variety of crimes including robbery, burglary, sexual assault and all types of white-collar crimes. Some of these crimes were worked in conjunction to other crimes, but I was challenged with working investigations. Unlike in the movies, a tremendous amount of time was spent writing reports, preparing cases and testifying in court.

The most intriguing cases of all of these were the homicides. We worked several serial murders during that time including William (Billy) Happ and Aileen Wuornos, a female serial killer. Happ was convicted of the murder of Angela Crowley and maintained his innocence up until moments before his execution, when he decided to confess. Aileen Wuornos killed seven men in five different counties, including forty-three-year-old David Spears, whose body was found in our county. She too was executed after being convicted of six murders. Her lover, Tyria Moore, was able to engage her in recorded conversation while she was in jail, and she eventually confessed to all of the murders. Eileen's entire life was one of tragedy. She was apparently beaten and raped as a child and turned to prostitution at age eleven. Many times, the anti-social behavior of many criminals can be traced back to their environment, background and family life as a child. This, however, cannot be used as an alibi for murder. Justice must prevail.

CHAPTER 31
GOING HOME

S usan and I both grew up in Alabama, and we had longed for the right opportunity to return. While on a hunting trip, a good friend of mine, Larry Martin, who was Police Chief in Mt. Vernon, told me they were advertising for a new Police Chief in Bay Minette, Alabama. I called Bay Minette City Hall and was told they currently had about one hundred and thirty-five applicants, but I could submit my resume if I chose to do so. I thought to myself, "What have I got to lose?" I submitted my resume and shortly thereafter was contacted for an interview. I was called back for a second interview; and at this point, Susan and I began to discuss the what ifs. To complicate things even more, in the interim I received a letter from The Florida Department of Law Enforcement (F.D.L.E.) offering me a position as a Special Agent. Knowing that most new agents had to start in places like Miami or Jacksonville, I was less than enthused about the possibility.

Susan and I talked and decided to lay out a fleece, as they did in the Bible. We prayed and said if Bay Minette calls and offers me a specific amount of money, that I would take the job. On a Wednesday evening, Mayor Ricky Rhodes called and offered the exact amount of money we had specified in our prayers. I accepted the job immediately. I worked out a notice at Citrus County, and with a combination of regrets and sadness, I made arrangements to leave. It was not easy to leave friends that I had worked with over the years. These were people I had backed up on many occasions, and they had been there for me. Many of them had camped out in the hallway of the hospital after I was shot. They were a special group of people, and many are still our friends to this day. I cherish the many good times we had together. We looked forward to a new chapter in our lives, but our leaving Citrus County was bittersweet.

Trying to transition from a large sheriff's department in Florida to a small police department in Alabama was not an easy task. My daughter, Amy, decided to come with me to Alabama, and Susan remained in Florida in order to let Brooke finish the school year, and to try and get the house sold and our belongings packed. Our oldest daughter, Bridget, was already in college. A very gracious, retired couple, Larry and Elizabeth Duryea, allowed Amy and me to live in their guest house until we could make other living arrangements.

My first week on the job was quite entertaining. Traveling back from the middle of town back to the police department, I passed a man on a bicycle headed in the opposite direction. Upon arriving at the department, I told the dispatcher, Buford Biggs, what I had observed. I said the man looked like one of our prisoners in the jail. Buford said, "Oh yeah that's old Luke. We let him out about once a week to go to K-Mart to do his shopping for snacks and underwear and stuff." Buford told me not to worry, because he always comes back. I immediately thought about Otis on the Andy Griffith Show. That same week I was in City Hall when a man came in screaming. There was another man close behind with an unfolded pocket knife in his hand. I grabbed the second man as he was yelling, "I'm gonna cut your throat." It seems that the first man had done something inappropriate to the second man's niece, or that is what I could understand. These were some of the more humorous things which occurred, but were in no way a reflection of the majority of people in town.

With a new Police Chief in town, there was much skepticism, both from within the department, and within the community. Growing up in South Alabama, I saw myself as coming back home, but many viewed me as an outsider, and I knew I would have to prove my worth, both to the officers and to the people in town. Everyone was very friendly, but many kept their distance. I had to take a written exam, a physical endurance test and qualify with a firearm in order to transfer my police standards certification from Florida.

Van Davis, the head of the local police academy, which was located at Faulkner Community College in Bay Minette, was very helpful in my accomplishing this.

I prayed for God's favor upon me and my family in our new surroundings, that the people and the officers would have confidence in me and my ability to lead the department, and that they would know I could be trusted. It wasn't long before there were two incidents which helped in this transition.

CHAPTER 32
THE JAIL BREAK

»»»

At that time, the police department was located right next to the Baldwin County Sheriff's Department on one side and the City Fire Department on the other side. One day while several of the officers and I were talking in the patrol room, a fireman rushed in through the back door and said there had been a jail break. The Sheriff's department had an exercise yard out in the back which had a twelve-foot fence with razor wire over the top. Three prisoners, who were out in the yard, had climbed the fence, thrown their jackets on top of the razor wire, and climbed over the fence. There was a wooded area about two blocks large that they had entered running on foot.

Several of my officers had entered the woods, at that point, with guns drawn, giving chase. I had one of the officers, Jimmy Ferguson, drive me around to the other side of the wooded area where I got out with Jimmy's shot gun and waited. To complicate matters even more, there were several inhabited houses located there, and the Elementary School was across the street.

Not knowing why, the prisoners were in jail, possibly murder.... or even crimes against children, I knew I could not allow them to get to the elementary school. The children and teachers became my first priority. As I waited, I could hear men yelling out in the woods, so I continued to wait. Suddenly one of the prisoners came running out, and as he did, I racked a round of buck shot into the twelve-gauge pump shotgun. I yelled out, "Stop or I'll shoot!" He looked at me like he wasn't quite sure if I was serious, and I said, "If you take another step, I'll shoot!" With this last command we got him to lay down on the ground, and Jimmy cuffed him. Suddenly the second one came out of the woods, and I gave him the same command. He didn't seem to take me seriously and lifted his foot to run again. At this point I said. "If you take one more step, you're a dead man!" Amusingly, he stood with one foot still in the air. I suppose he decided I was serious. We had him lay down and cuffed him also. While this was taking place, the third man had crawled under one of the houses, but one of the deputies crawled under and got him out.

All three prisoners had been captured. Hoss Mack, the current Baldwin County Sheriff, who was an investigator at the time told me later I had a new nick-name. When he interviewed the prisoners later, they all referred to me as "Shotgun." Some may wonder, would I have actually shot those men? The answer is yes. Not because I wanted to, but not knowing their charges, I could not take the chance on them creating a hostage situation with the school children. The Elementary School was just across the street from where they were captured. In law enforcement we are many times put in situations where we have no time to analyze the situation, but rather we have to make split second decisions based on our training and instincts. In this situation, no one was harmed and I thank God for that.

CHAPTER 33
CAPITAL MURDER IN BAY MINETTE ALABAMA

»»»

R aymond Giadrosich was a thirty-seven-year-old man with a very strong and angry temperament. Some said they were fearful of him, because they thought he was crazy. Others said, he would fight you if he was angered. Either way, most people did not feel comfortable with him. I would have liked to have interviewed his wife Sandra and listened to her comments about Raymond's temper, but Raymond denied me the chance of ever doing that. Raymond had agreed to meet with his thirty-four-year-old wife, Sandra, and her fifty-five-year-old mother, Ruby Cobb, at the law offices of Bayless Byles across the street from the Baldwin County Court House.

It was around noon on a warm summer day, and there had been a power failure in town. Many people were coming out of the courthouse for lunch. Others were leaving businesses in town. There was nothing unusual about this day, except for one thing. Raymond was on a mission. This was a mission he had planned for several days, if not weeks. He and Sandra had four children together, and Raymond did not want to grant her the divorce which she was adamantly seeking. He had decided there would be only one way to settle this matter. We do not know, nor shall we ever know just how far Raymond intended to go with this mission of death, so I will only describe the things that we do know, and the rest can be left to speculation.

In anticipation of his meeting with Sandra, Raymond had borrowed a 30.06 hunting rifle. He had gone to a store and purchased a box of ammunition for the rifle. The four children had been left with Raymond's mother at the Continental Apartments while the meeting was taking place at the lawyer's office. During the meeting Attorney Byles described Raymond as being very agreeable about the terms of the divorce, even agreeing to allow Sandra to keep custody of the children. He was so agreeable, that I believe this frightened Sandra. I believe she sensed that something wasn't right. Upon leaving the attorney's office, Raymond asked Sandra and her mother to meet him at his mother's apartment to see the children. She refused.

It was at this point that Raymond became very angry, and an argument ensued, Sandra had refused to comply with what Raymond was demanding, and this infuriated him. Witnesses said they could see them arguing in the parking lot. Sandra came back into the attorney's office and told Vicky, Attorney Byles' legal assistant, that Raymond was demanding that they meet him at his mother's apartment. Vicky advised her not to go, and told her not to go back out there. For whatever reason, Sandra returned to the parking lot. Suddenly in a calm and deliberate manner, Raymond walked over to his car and took the loaded and chambered rifle off of the back seat. In terror, Sandra began running back toward the lawyer's office. Raymond shot her once, and she fell through the front door. She probably died immediately. Ruby Cobb also had begun to run and Raymond shot her once, and she fell dead in front of her car.

The women inside of the law office were terrified and thought they might become his next victims. They ran to the conference room and hid under a table. Raymond was an accomplished hunter. He had probably killed many deer in this same way, using this same kind of ammunition. This time, however, the hunt was different. He had just killed two innocent people, and no one will ever know what his intentions had been if they had agreed to meet at his mother's apartment. No one knows what might have happened next had God not placed me very strategically where He did on that particular day.

I was about six blocks away when I heard the shots. Having hunted quite a bit myself, I was pretty sure that I heard rifle shots. What I did not know was where the shots had come from or the carnage which had taken place. I drove slowly toward the center of town. There had been a power outage about noon that day, and many people were leaving the court house and witnessed the mayhem not far away. Raymond, on the other hand, was described by witnesses to turn the rifle in the direction of those people leaving the court house, causing them to run in every direction. A witness said he reloaded the rifle, placed it back on the back seat of the car, and slowly got in and drove away. He was headed toward the apartments where his mother and children were located. We will probably never know what his intentions were once he arrived. Still looking for answers, I turned left on to Fourth Street, about two blocks from where the shootings had taken place. From the opposite direction I saw another car turning on to Fourth Street heading toward me very slowly. Now at this point, I must inject this unbelievable statement. What are the chances that Raymond and I would be turning on to the same street at the same time? What are the chances that I would pull in front of his vehicle and stop him, if it were not for God's intercession? That is exactly what happened. I got out of my vehicle, unarmed and approached Raymond on the driver's side window. The window was down. I was just about to ask if he had heard any shots, or where they might have come from, when Raymond noticed the badge I was wearing on my hip.

CAPITAL MURDER IN BAY MINETTE ALABAMA

He made a spontaneous statement. He looked up at me with his cold brown eyes and said. "I just killed my wife and my mother-in-law." My only response was, "Okay." I opened Raymond's car door, pulled him out on the street, and wedged him under the car door on the asphalt while I retrieved my handcuffs from my car. I didn't talk to him or ask him any questions. I had one of my officers transport him to my office with the instructions that he was to be carefully guarded, and no one was to talk to him until I arrived.

After having Raymond transported to the office, I then went to the crime scene. There was mass chaos at the scene. E.M.T.s had now arrived, and they were working feverishly to resuscitate the two victims. Both were transported to the hospital, where they were pronounced dead on arrival. One investigator went to the hospital in case either victim survived long enough to make a statement. Another investigator was charged with processing evidence at the scene, and another with taking crime scene photographs. All investigators at the scene were charged with interviewing witnesses and taking their statements.

After making assignments, I returned to my office. Upon arrival, I advised Raymond Giadrosich of his constitutional rights and after he waived his rights, I began to talk with him. Raymond gave me a detailed, taped confession which I played for the jury during his trial. He broke down several times during his confession, which made me think in his own way, he may have been sorry for what had happened.

In one of the most unusual verdicts in history, Raymond was found guilty of murdering his wife, and not guilty, by reason of insanity, in the death of his mother-in-law. Both murders occurred within seconds of each other, and yet there were two completely contradictive verdicts. He is currently serving a life sentence for murder, and upon release should be transported to a Mental Health facility.

As horrific as this case was, I am thankful that it was not worse. This case went a long way toward helping to solidify my place within the department and in the community.

CHAPTER 34
WHO IS THE DEVIL ANYWAY?

》》》

To say we had a diverse group of inmates in our jail is probably an understatement. Some were such frequent visitors that they would sometimes start to homestead or take up residence. One, who I will call Buddy, would, while under the influence, take on the persona of a Celestial Being at times. He would tell me, "Chief, you can't do anything to me because I am Jesus Christ." Other times he would threaten me by telling me he was Satan, and he could do whatever he wanted. Neither of these imagined personalities could figure out a way to get out of jail, but the dialogue was quite humorous at times.

On one occasion, I heard that Buddy had shot a man up in the Perdido area. This was a Sheriff's Department case, but we often backed them up on cases, so I decided to go to that area and look for Buddy, hoping if I found him, I might be able to talk him in to giving up his shotgun without incident. While driving down a dirt road, I noticed what I will call a pig trail between two pine trees and what appeared to be tire tracks. As I started down the trail in my car, I looked up ahead about fifty yards and spotted a full sized, older vehicle that looked like Buddy's car. Buddy was standing outside on the passenger side of the car. Even though I did not see a weapon, I knew Buddy could pull one out fairly quickly, and I did not know what Buddy's state of mind might be. I left my vehicle and walked down the trail with my weapon in my hand, but behind me. As I got closer, I engaged in conversation with Buddy. I asked if he had a weapon, and he told me there was a shotgun on the back seat. It was a hot, summer day and the windows were down on his vehicle. I reached in through the window and retrieved the shotgun while keeping an eye on Buddy. I didn't know if he had any other weapons with him. At this point, I told Buddy I had been looking for him. Very calmly Buddy said, "Why you lookin for me?" I told Buddy there was a man at the hospital suffering from shotgun wounds and that he had alleged that Buddy had shot him. Buddy asked, "Is this the same man who molested my fourteen-year-old niece?" I told Buddy I didn't know anything about the molestation, but I was going to have to take him in. Handcuffed and in the car, Buddy reiterated that he had not shot anyone. At this point, Buddy made a very strange statement. He said he had been out in the woods shooting snakes. He went on to say if he had shot at a snake in a palmetto bush and someone happened to be behind the bush and got hit, then it was their own fault. Enough said.

CHAPTER 35
SETTLING IN
AS POLICE CHIEF

»»»

There was much to be done as the new Police Chief. The only weapons that the department had issued were a few outdated and barely functional shotguns. There was much training that was needed, but I had inherited a good group of seasoned and experienced officers who just needed some direction. Mayor Rhodes along with the City Council, were very supportive of the police department.

I thought it was going to be a good fit, not only for me, but for my family also. I worried about how the transition would affect them. My daughter, Amy, had just made cheerleader again in Florida, but she had chosen to come with me to Bay Minette. On her second day of school in Bay Minette, she tried out and made the cheerleading squad. I was so thankful for this. Everything seemed to be falling into place, and I knew God was very much directing our path. Susan, my wife, had a lot of pressure on her. She stayed behind so Brooke, our youngest daughter, could finish out the school year. Hopefully, we would all be reunited soon. Our daughter, Bridget, who was already in college in Florida, eventually moved to Alabama, and our family unit was now, once again, complete.

CHAPTER 36
MURDER WHEN YOU LEAST EXPECT IT

»»»

It was a typical day in the town of Bay Minette. The weather was cool, and people were rushing around getting ready for Christmas. It was business as usual at lunch that day in Street's Restaurant. Eugene Overstreet, a Vietnam vet, who lost a leg during the war, had opened his restaurant some years before and enjoyed a thriving lunch business. Many of the locals stopped by for lunch and to feast on an all you can eat buffet. The conversations ranged anywhere from college football to politics and back to football. There was always a local flavor to both the politics and the football.

There were several interesting characters living in Bay Minette, and in the surrounding area. One was a lady named Gertrude. Now Gertrude lived in the Pine Grove area and was a fixture in the City of Bay Minette. She always rode a bicycle and would come up to locals asking them for change. Usually she asked, "You got a quarter?" Most people would reward her, but some would just tell her, "No!" Those who knew her story said she didn't have to beg but chose to do so. Gertrude was mentally challenged. I never knew what she did with all of that silver, but she managed to acquire a lot. On one occasion, Eugene said she came into the Restaurant and was using a screwdriver to try and break in to some of the vending machines. When Eugene threatened to report her to the Mayor, he said she danced a jig away from him while making a lewd motion with her middle finger. Eugene had pity for Gertrude and would take her home on many occasions when it was raining. There were other characters around town including Donald and Peelicker. I don't know how Peelicker acquired his nickname, nor did I believe I wanted to know.

Another fixture at Street's was an older gentleman named Moody Ray Knight. Moody Ray was a very boisterous man who was very opinionated about most things. He loved to flirt with the waitresses at Streets and one in particular named Barbara. He liked to carry around a lot of money in cash, and many commented that this would get him in trouble one day. Barbara said Moody Ray was always buying her gifts and proposed marriage on several occasions. Moody Ray was partially paralyzed on one side and walked with a cane in order to steady himself. His home was a neat, brick structure surrounded by a chain link fence in a very quiet neighborhood.

It was cold in Bay Minette on this December night with Christmas on the horizon. Moody Ray was in his bed fast asleep and anticipating the next day like most of us around town. Persons unknown went to Moody Ray's house on this night, cut the phone line and the power and broke in through the rear. They accomplished this by breaking out a glass window. What transpired at this point, we will probably never know. We think Moody Ray woke up, fought and struggled with his attackers, but he was beaten severely. He was discovered the next morning by his son-in-law nearly dead and suffering from exposure. He laid on the cold floor for hours before his discovery. The crime scene was very contaminated by family members and paramedics prior to our arrival. Clarence Crook, one of the city's investigators, collected evidence from the scene which was transported to the forensic lab. At the hospital I, along with Moody Ray's grandson, Warren, attempted to question Moody Ray about his attackers. The only information we could get was that there were two of them, and they were black. We realized we were looking for a needle in a hay stack, but I had been in that position before. Moody Ray lingered for several days, but he finally succumbed to the beating and the exposure. A few days after Christmas, Moody Ray passed away. We were now looking for two murderers.

Nothing that we sent to the forensic lab proved to be of evidentiary value. We knew we had to get a lead, and we needed to find some physical evidence. Clarence went to work talking to people while Kenneth Hall, Jimmy Franklin, Roland Howell, and I searched the house and the yard looking for anything that could be evidence. In investigation, everything is important until it can be ruled out. Roland discovered a cigarette butt in the grass beside the house. Upon further examination, we saw it was a Cool Cigarette–which Moody Ray did not smoke. With Moody Ray's yard being fenced, we knew whoever left the butt there had to have traversed the fence. In addition, it was close to where the phone lines had been cut and the power shut off. Roland placed the butt in evidence and it was sent to the forensic lab to see if they could extract DNA.

Days went by with no leads. For the most part the family was being very helpful and understanding. The community had started to demand answers. This was not unusual. People were afraid. They knew a killer, or possibly more than one, was walking around loose among them. They wondered who would be next. I received the normal phone calls in a situation like this. People were asking, "Do you think it could be so and so, or maybe so and so?" Law enforcement experiences two types of pressure at a time like that: the pressure that a fearful public place on us, and the pressure we place on ourselves. Everyone wants the case solved, but we know that it is up to us to solve it.

Finally, we got a break. Someone gave Clarence Crook information that Robert Taylor, Junior… aka Little Rabbit, may have something to do with it. Little Rabbit was well known to law enforcement, but he had never done anything of this magnitude. We brought him in for questioning, and Clarence and I interrogated him for over an hour. While we did not get a confession, we did get enough information to lead us to believe he was involved. His body language told me that he was lying, and this was enough for us to order a DNA sample from him. The investigation was starting to come together.

Within a few short weeks after the murder we received word from the lab. The DNA on the cigarette butt matched the DNA of Little Rabbit. Now it was time for some serious interrogation. Armed with the new evidence, Clarence and I once again conducted an interrogation with Little Rabbit. After a while he broke and began to tell us the whole story. He said he, Lucius, and Aretha had come up with the plan. (Lucius and Aretha are not their real names, but I have changed their names, because they were never convicted of the murder.) He said Aretha stood guard outside while he and Lucius broke in the house. The motive for the break-in was robbery. Once inside Moody Ray awoke and began to attack them with his cane. It is unclear who actually administered the beating, but both parties probably did it.

We tried to get a confession from Lucius, but he was very street savvy and would not budge. The same with Aretha. Now the only thing tying the two of them to the case was the testimony of Little Rabbit, and that was not enough. The District Attorney refused to prosecute based solely on a co-defendant's testimony. Lucius made one crucial mistake, however. He was on federal parole at the time, and he had sold Moody Ray's pocket knife to a pawn shop. This very unusual pocket knife was identified by various family members, and with the help of Donna Dobbins, an Assistant U.S. Attorney, they were able to revoke his parole and send him back to Federal Prison. Aretha was never convicted, but all she did was stand guard. Little Rabbit received a life sentence, and is still in prison to this day.

CHAPTER 37
THE CASE THAT ROCKED AN ENTIRE COMMUNITY

»»»

For the most part, living in the sleepy, little town of Bay Minette would be considered boring in the opinion of some people. While we experienced the same types of criminal activity that you find in many small towns, most of the time; things were pretty casual and sedate. A normal day for me involved stopping off in the morning for a cup of coffee and then heading in to the office before eight. There we would make another pot of coffee, and I would sit around in the lobby with my secretary, Gloria, and other officers who might be on duty that day, and discuss and laugh over different topics of conversation about the job or unrelated things. Patsy, the Court Magistrate would sometimes join us, as well as Deputy Chief Kenny Hall, Lt. Jimmy Franklin and Lt. Roland Howell. The officers who were on duty that day would sometimes join us, if they were not busy on calls. Life was good. I loved my job, and I loved being where I was. However, something was about to happen that would rock the whole community. Because of the sensitivity of the crimes committed, the names of the victims have been changed, in order to protect their reputation and privacy.

It was late at night when I received the call. Ms. Lavenia Stockdale, a retired, widowed school teacher had reported that someone had broken into her home and raped her. We, along with the sheriff's department, had responded to the scene and were working the case. Ms. Lavenia was a very beloved, God fearing woman in her late eighties. It was hard to believe that anyone would do such a thing. Why would a young man choose such a defenseless, elderly lady? There were very few clues other than DNA from the semen recovered at the hospital when the doctor performed a rape kit. We had very few leads. We only knew the suspect's race, approximate age, body build and physical characteristics. We figured he had stalked the victim and knew she would be alone in the home, because her son lived less than a hundred yards away. We did not know how he got there. Was there an accomplice who dropped him off?

Many questions were not answered at that time. The most glaring question was, of course, would there be others, or was this an isolated incident? That question would be answered several days later, and the answer would send shock waves throughout the community.

The next victim fit the pattern and time frame of the previous one. It was late at night. She was an elderly, white woman who lived alone in a relatively isolated location, and she was awakened by the intruder and sexually assaulted. The suspect always carried a pocket knife and threatened violence if they did not cooperate. Our worse fears had been realized. We now had a serial rapist.

The community was outraged and scared. I began to hear questions like: When are you going to catch this guy? Are you guys capable of doing your job? I completely understood. People were frightened and feared for their loved ones. Little did we know that things would get much worse before getting any better. Two of the next victims were younger. One of the young women was able to fight off his attack. She provided a pretty accurate description of the attacker, but there were still no leads.

The other young woman had a small baby in the house. She told me she allowed him to rape her because she feared that if she didn't, he might harm her baby, and she just wanted him to hurry and leave. The rapist had now changed his motive of operation when he selected younger victims. The only additional leads we had were the description of a vehicle which was a small green car and a red plaid, flannel shirt which he wore during most of the crimes.

We had started to figure out several things about the perpetrator. We knew that he was probably working alone, and that he was a black male in his late thirties to early forties. He was short, approximately five feet seven or eight. He spoke very articulately, and he had a husky, muscular build. He usually wore a red flannel shirt, and he drove a green car. We figured he either worked or lived in the southeast portion of Bay Minette or in the Pine Grove area. His victims were all white, and appeared to be randomly selected because of their being alone and mostly vulnerable. The attacks happened usually three days to a week apart. Our concerns were that he might decide to start killing victims. I had never dealt with a case quite like this one. Many times, I prayed for God to help us resolve this case. I didn't care who might receive the credit. We just needed it to stop. Many nights I went out on my own and ride the area looking for a suspect. I would pray as I drove. Father, I would pray, we need your help, and we need some relief from this awful situation which has fallen upon our community.

Another major concern was that we started to notice a number of vigilantes riding around in trucks, armed to the hilt with shotguns and hunting rifles. We usually stopped them and encouraged them to go home. We now had the additional problem of some well-meaning person taking a shot at the first black person they saw in an all -white neighborhood. We did not think this would happen, but tensions were running high, and who knows what someone might do, especially if alcohol were involved. Let me say that there were very few race problems in Bay Minette, and we certainly did not want any to start.

Bonnie Lou Jones lived in a very modest white wooden home next to the railroad track. She was in her mid-seventies and had never married. She was devoted to taking care of her invalid mother who was almost ninety years old. She was very active in her church and was loved by everyone. Her whole world would change on one dark, summer night. Bonnie Lou was awakened by an intruder. He raped her while her invalid mother watched from her bed. Unable to help her daughter, she cried and pled with the man to stop, but he did not. The excitement of being able to accomplish this in front of her mother probably motivated him even more. The depravity of this man's sick mind had no equal. He could have easily closed the mother's bedroom door, but he wanted her to watch as he raped and brutalized her daughter on the couch in front of her.

We thought we had our first major lead in the case. When I questioned Bonnie Lou as to whether or not she recognized the man, she initially hesitated. She said she did not have on her glasses, and it had been very dark; however, she said from the sound of his voice, she believed it was a man who did her yard work. We immediately began to focus on John Barns, the yard man. She further stated that she could smell gasoline on his hands, which was consistent with someone who worked on/with lawn-mowers. Things seemed to be coming together. I believed that maybe our prayers were being answered.

We picked up John Barnes. I began to interrogate him and found that he was married with several children. I also realized that I had been called to his residence several years before when he had a baby who died from a SIDS death. He was unable to give an alibi on the night of the assault. When questioned separately, his wife stated that there had been many nights when he had gone out without explanation, and she did not know where he had been. She said she thought he had been doing something he shouldn't have. John fit the physical description, and he was very well-spoken. This appeared to fit everything we were searching for, and we had a victim who had identified him. He was very cooperative, and when we asked him for a blood sample; he consented.

Everything seemed to be falling into place. Larry Milstid, Chief Deputy for the Sheriff's Department, and I waited impatiently for a call from the forensic lab, and finally the call came. The lady on the line said, "You've got your man!" She said the first strand of DNA came back positive, and they had never had the first strain to be positive and the rest of the test to be negative.

We were now faced with a dilemma. Should we wait for the final test to come back before we made an arrest? We had released John Barnes, and if we waited, there was a possibility he might strike again. Law enforcement is challenged with many difficult decisions, and this was one of the hardest. Chief Milstid and I agreed. We must go ahead and make the arrest. We arrested John Barnes on a bench warrant from the Judge after we both swore in an affidavit to his guilt.

We held a press conference to announce that the serial rapist had been arrested. The community could now relax. We, in law enforcement, could now get some needed rest. Everything was beginning to get back to normal, and then it happened! The phone call from the lab….. They had been wrong. The second strand of DNA came back negative. We had arrested the wrong man! Had we been too impulsive? I have thought about this many times over the years, and I believe, if faced with the same set of circumstances again and with the information we had; I would probably do the same thing. With the information I now have, I would have waited before making the arrest. In all of my years of law enforcement, this would be the only time I have known that I arrested the wrong man. We tried to set the record straight. I personally apologized to John Barns and his family, and we held another press conference to let the world know of our mistake. This was a very humbling ordeal for both Larry and me. However, we had to do the right thing.

We were back to square one. There was still a serial rapist loose in our community, and he must be stopped. I was hurt, embarrassed, and starting to question my own ability as an investigator. I did not have time to wallow in my own self-pity. I went back to God looking for answers. I think sometimes God allows things like this to happen in order to check our own abilities and confidence so we will realize that whatever ability we may have has been given to us by Him. In other words, I may have been too full of myself. This was a humbling experience for me.

We had brought in two Alabama Bureau of Investigation Agents to work with us on this case. Bob Scheer and Don Tucker were both seasoned investigators, and at this point; we needed all the help we could get.

There was a lady in the Pine Grove area who the perpetrator had raped twice. He actually came back a second time and broke into her house and raped her. I had begun to panic a little bit. I knew God was in control, but we were under tremendous pressure from the community to solve this case. There may have been more self-imposed pressure than external. Once again, I prayed, "God, I don't care who gets the credit, please just allow this case to be resolved."

Suddenly one day, the break came that we so desperately needed. Don and Bob were standing on the front porch conducting an interview with the victim who had been raped twice; when a man drove by in a small green car who physically fit the description of the offender. The man was driving slowly and was looking intently at what was taking place on the porch. The two agents followed him to his location at a local well-drilling place in Pine Grove. They asked him to submit to being fingerprinted and ultimately, they were able to match his prints with a print that had been lifted at the house where the woman was raped twice. Anthony McCants was arrested, and a sample of DNA was retrieved from hair follicles. This time the DNA was a match. We had our guy, and the case was solved. The community could now breathe a collective sigh of relief. I later went on a search warrant to Anthony McCants' home, and when I looked in his clothes closet, I discovered the red plaid shirt which he had worn in most of the attacks. We had a very solid case. McCants went to trial, was convicted on multiple counts of rape, attempted rape, sexual assault, burglary and robbery. He was sentenced to 999 years in prison and still remains there to this day.

CHAPTER 38
FACE TO FACE WITH A MIRACLE

»»»

There have been times in my life when I questioned whether or not God was with me. I never questioned His existence, but like a lot of people, I would not feel his presence, and therefore wasn't quite sure whether He was concerned about me in particular. Did He hear me each time I prayed? After all, could the ruler of the universe actually have time to listen to what I had to say? Many of us, I'm sure, have struggled with these thoughts.

Every now and then I have had God manifest himself to me in miraculous ways. Let me qualify these remarks by saying that it has nothing to do with my being special. I am so far removed from that. I believe it has more to do with my being willing to listen and then being obedient to do what He tells me to do.

It was a bleak overcast day when I left for Pensacola one fall afternoon. I had enrolled in graduate school at Troy University and was taking classes in Public Administration at the Troy Campus of the Pensacola Naval Air Station. When I arrived at the building where my class was located it had already started raining slightly. The wind was blowing and it was very dark overhead. Wearing a white dress shirt and tie, I got out of my brand-new white Ford Crown Victoria and opened my umbrella while I loaded up my books. As I started to walk away, a young sailor walked by and said, "You have a tire going flat on the left rear of your car." I thanked him and thought to myself, "I'll stop and get some air after class." As I walked toward my classroom, I was thinking to myself how odd it was for the tire to be low on air. After all, the city had just purchased the car for me and it was a brand-new tire. Several hours later, upon leaving class, it was now storming. The wind was blowing fiercely, and water was several inches deep in the parking lot. When I arrived at my car, I became very upset. The tire was completely flat. I got out my new spare tire and began the arduous task of changing the tire. Ever tried changing a tire in a monsoon with dress clothes on? It was a recipe for disaster. Eventually the rain blew my umbrella inside out. Frustrated, I threw it down on the ground and finished changing the tire. I was dirty, drenched with rain, running about twenty minutes late, and I sat there in my car, wallowing in despair and anxious to take this out on someone.

Now it was God's turn. I asked God why He would allow something so sinister to happen to me. Wasn't this a brand new car with brand new tires? Why did it happen in the middle of a rain storm? There were hundreds of cars in that parking area, and I didn't notice any other cars with flat tires. Was I being punished? God did not respond, and I don't believe I expected him to.

After composing myself, I left…..heading home. As I would sometimes do, I exited off of the Interstate to take the shortcut through the forest. Along this desolate stretch of road, you would sometimes go for miles without seeing a light or a house. It was still raining, and I saw what appeared to be an old passenger van up ahead on the shoulder of the road. This area was known to be frequented by drug dealers, and most civilians would never stop; but being armed and with a police radio, I felt comfortable, so I pulled up next to the van. Letting down my passenger side window, the driver began to lower his window also. He began to relate a very amazing story. He said he was a youth minister at a church in Pensacola, and he had been headed to Bay Minette to speak at the Juvenile Detention Center. To make matters worse, he had a young man with him who was a paraplegic in a wheelchair. He said his transmission had gone out. He could not push the young man down the side of the highway in the dark and with it raining. He said he was afraid to leave him there while he walked to get help. They had no cell phone. He said we did the only thing we knew to do, and that was to pray. I asked how long they had been sitting there and he said, "About fifteen minutes." I called and arranged for someone to come from Pensacola to get them.

Afterwards, as I headed home, I started to think, now they had been sitting there for fifteen minutes. The flat tire had delayed me about twenty minutes. Had it not been for the flat tire, I would have already gone by before they broke down. Some may say the above incident was nothing more than a coincidence.

The next day I took the tire to Brantley Tires to get it repaired. I told Thomas Brantley the tire must have something in it, because it went flat very quickly. Thomas put fifty pounds of air in the tire and submerged it in a vat full of water. There were no air bubbles, and there was no leak. He put the tire back on the car, and it never leaked down again.

God knew everything which would take place that evening, and was answering that young preacher's prayer... even hours before he prayed. Wow! I was filled with joy and thankfulness that God allowed me to be a part of what had just taken place.

CHAPTER 39
IN HIS HANDS

»»»

I consider myself to be a very ordinary man. Having no visions of grandeur, I realize that there are many people in this world who are much smarter, better looking, more informed and better educated than I am. The fact that God has chosen to use me on certain occasions to affect His will, puts me in the same class as the donkey and the axe. They too had little value until God used them. You see, I believe God likes to choose, "the least of these," so no one will question who is in control. Being one of the, "the least of these," is the category I fall into.

Another thing God likes is to find people who are willing to listen to His voice, and obey His instruction. This is something I strive to do every day. On many occasions I have felt that I was in His hands, just as I was on the night of the shootout.......even when I was not aware of it at the time.

I am so humbled that God has allowed me to experience so much, and so thankful for the many blessings He has given me and my family. We serve an awesome God, and God is good.

Jeremiah 29:11

For I know the thoughts that I think toward you, says the Lord, thoughts of peace and not of evil, to give you a future and a hope. (NKJV)

REFLECTIONS

>> >> >>

A ccomplishing a dream is rare—-and awesome. Many people attempt to write a book, but statistics tell us only a few ever succeed.

You have accomplished your dream and made your goal a reality! I am so happy and proud for you, because I know how tirelessly you've worked and how difficult it has been for you to re-live many of the emotional memories and life shattering situations you've encountered during this exciting journey!

I feel blessed to be a part of your life. I know our children and grandchildren will read and reread this book for many years to come. What a legacy you will leave for them and many others in future years, because you have captured your deepest emotions through this brilliantly written manuscript.

I love you and wish you much success. You did it!
Congratulations.........Love, Susan

James Strickland "might have felt he met his match" after a deputy wounded him four times, the medical examiner said.

By GEORGE WILKENS
Tribune Staff Writer

INVERNESS — James Dennis Strickland died from a self-inflicted shot into his right temple, not from four gunshot wounds fired by a Citrus County deputy, a medical examiner said Thursday.

An autopsy performed Wednesday showed four of six shots fired by Citrus County Sheriff's Deputy Bruce Lovell hit their mark, striking Strickland in the right thigh, left buttock and twice in the left arm, said Dr. James C. Niliner, associate medical examiner for the 5th Judicial Circuit.

Niliner said Strickland would have survived all four wounds, although he deemed one arm wound a serious one that probably rendered Strickland's gun hand useless. "He might have felt he met his match."

James Strickland

OCALA ★ ST[A]

Shooting Victim Was Murderer

By KEITH MORELLI
Citrus County Bureau

INVERNESS — A man killed after a shootout with a Citrus County deputy late Tuesday night has been identified as a convicted murderer and bank robber, who apparently was hiding in a mobile home to avoid police seeking him in a second killing.

The victim, James Dennis Strickland, 38, whose last known address was Pompano Beach, was on parole for the bank robbery and was in the vacant mobile home in Citronelle when the deputy spotted him.

Deputy Bruce Lovett ordered the man out of the mobile home, but the suspect broke through the rear

Citrus Times — DAVE MORRISO

Deputy honored for outstanding service

Citrus County Sheriff's Deputy Bruce Lovett received a resolution from the Citrus County Commission Tuesday honoring him for "outstanding service in the line of duty." Lovett, 35, was shot five times Aug. 10 after he responded to a prowler call near Crytal River. His assailant, who was wanted for murder in Broward County, killed himself. Lovett spent about two weeks in the hospital and returned

Citrus County Sheriff's Department

§ Presents the Medal of Valor to §

Bruce Lovett

In recognition of his performance of an act of extreme heroism while engaged in personal combat with an armed adversary at imminent personal hazard of life in the performance of duty.

Issued this ___4th___ day of ___December___ 19 83

CHARLES S. DEAN, Citrus County Sheriff

Sheriff Charles Dean presenting me with certificate for the
Legion of Honor at the National Police Hall of Fame.

Citrus agents help with big Tampa bust

By JOHN D. McKINNON
Citrus Times Staff Writer

INVERNESS — The Citrus County sheriff's special drug investigations unit got a taste of the big time early Wednesday morning as agents helped Tampa and federal officials make nine arrests and seize about three tons of marijuana.

Tampa police are terming the case their biggest marijuana bust in the past five years.

"It was exciting," said Sgt. Bruce Lovett after the unit members returned to Citrus County late Wednesday after two days in Tampa. Part of that time was spent undercover helping federal officials and Tampa police set up and then bust nine persons who will be charged with trafficking.

Mrs. Ogles found dec

Body found in woods; sheriff tight-lipped

rs. Ogles at
, just after
office of the
motive was
her to an
trus Springs
ounty, and
the end of a
id set up to

tled, and he
nd then left,
hours later,
of the storm
oad.
her with his
r dead. She
t to a got in
r body was

forced Mrs.
access code
OR bankcard,
hed car and
o Ocal. He
tions would be
went to kala
elson d and
but heldn't
dy then. He

Times photo — KAREN SA

ane where Mrs. Ogles was taken.

St. Petersburg
citrus time
EDITION

Inverness — Crystal River — St. Petersburg, Fla.

An officer's intuition pays off

'Hunch' led chief investigator in the Ogles murder case to question Scott Weiand

By CHARLIE GOFEN
Times Staff Writer

INVERNESS — By mid-March, Citrus County Sheriff's Sgt. Bruce Lovett had spent more than two months investigating the murder of Gloria Lucille Ogles. The 54-year-old Crystal River woman had been abducted Jan. 6, and her body had been found 20 days later. An autopsy determined that she had been shot and strangled.

Lovett had witnesses' descriptions of a young man, and he had a long list of suspects, but he was nowhere close to solving the case.

So he prayed.

Lovett prayed at his Assembly of God church, he prayed while alone at his desk, and he prayed with another investigator on the case.

Then, after months of tenacious detective work, patience and faith, everything came together in a day.

The investigation that led to the arrest of Scott Brian Weiand in the Ogles murder case was a triumph for Lovett, but he is the first to say that it was not his case alone. Many officials in the department, including Sheriff Charles Dean, played instrumental roles in the investigation. And ultimately, Lovett said, much of his inspiration came from God.

Weiand has since been indicted by a grand jury on a charge of first-degree murder and is scheduled to go to trial Aug. 2, but prosecuting and defense attorneys say his case may end instead in a plea agreement.

• • •

At 7:25 p.m. on March 16, Citrus sheriff's investigator Marvin Padgett arrived at the McDonald's parking lot in Crystal River where he had arranged to meet with a young couple selling electronic's items.

Please see INTUITION Page 12

Tribune photo by GLEN STU...

Hit man allegedly sought

By CHRISTOPHER B. JONES
Times Staff Writer

Man accused of trying to hire gunman to kill 6

INVERNESS — The manager of a local sporting goods store has been accused of offering to hire a gunman to kill state Rep. Dick Locke, Circuit Judge William Edwards, Sheriff Charles Dean and three other Citrus County men.

Henry Malcolm Ayers, 53, the manager of Gator Sporting Goods in Crystal River, is being held without bail in Citrus County Jail on three counts of criminal solicitation to commit murder. His court appearance Thursday was in Brooksville because Edwards, the circuit court judge in Citrus County, allegedly was

undercover officer that he wanted to hire a hit man, according to sheriff's officials.

Ayers also targeted Larry Skidmore, owner of Skidmore's Sporting Goods, Ted Nipper, owner of Action Graphics, and Nipper's father, Fred Nipper, said Pat Fisher of the Sheriff's Office

Ayers took no other action against the six men, who were told of the threats against them Tuesday afternoon, Fisher said.

John Diner, who was in the store Thursday, said the charges "don't at all fit the character" of Ayers. "He's just as [...] 20 years. "He's just as [...]

"The first I heard about it was w Mrs. Ayers (Henry Ayers' wife) ca me Wednesday and said, 'We need a [...] gunner, and then I knew something [...] has worked in the store since it op [...] the early 1970s.

The Sheriff's Office got this [...] Authorities received a tip Tuesda concerned citizen" who said th "was looking to hire a gunman [...] six men. An undercover age Ayers, and the undercover [...] noon Wednesday in the parkin [...] front of the K mart store at Cr [...] At that meeting, [...] undercover officer agreed [...] Ayers agreed to pay the [...] til Skidmore and the Nip [...] he didn't have enough [...]

Judge gives rapist three life sentences

By BETTIE JOHNSON
Staff Writer

A 42-year-old Homosassa man was sentenced Friday to three consecutive life imprisonment terms after being found guilty of kidnapping and raping a 17-year-old girl last December.

Marion County Court Judge Hale Stancil sentenced Johnny Ingraham for two counts of sexual battery with threat of great force and kidnapping. He was also sentenced to two consecutive 30-year sentences on charges of sexual battery with slight force using a firearm.

That means after Ingraham serves the first life sentence, he faces two more, followed by 60 years in prison.

In addition, Ingraham was ordered to pay a total of $1,000 in court costs and a $2,500 public defender's lein.

The victim's mother, whose name is withheld to protect the identity of the girl, tearfully said she was happy with the sentence.

"As long as he's locked up forever," said the woman, who thanked jurors after they found Ingraham guilty of all charges but one (attempted sexual battery). "He doesn't need to be on the street. Each one of us is in danger.

Security was tight in the Ocala courtroom as Ingraham was fingerprinted. Seven bailiffs and two officers surrounded him [...] courtroom, spec [...] through a metal [...] scanned with [...] which

that the victim was a willing participant to the sexual act.

Assistant public defender Anthony Taiti argued told the jury the girl traded sex for cocaine.

Assistant state attorney Brad King debunked the defense's argument and enumerated contradictions in Ingraham's story.

"It takes no skill to look at the victim and see this is not a story she had weaved. She told the truth," King said.

Taking the witness stand Friday morning, Ingraham said the young girl called him at a Homosassa b [...] and asked him to meet her to sell h [...] some cocaine. Ingraham said he h [...] sold her the drug on prior occasio [...]

The young woman testified Th [...] day she had never seen Ingra [...] before the early morning hou [...] Dec. 17, when he passed her o [...] road, stopped, and forced he [...] the car.

The girl said she had b [...] boyfriend's house and was [...] four miles to a store to [...] mother to ask her to pick [...]

The girl said Ingraham [...] her by the hair, struck h [...] face, forced her to dis [...] threatened to shoot her if s [...] get out of the car.

He took her to a [...] mobile home, and force [...] repeated sex acts, sh [...] Throughout her eight-h [...] the girl said the gun [...] sight on a dresser top.

Thursday the girl had [...] tifying Ingraham, who [...] since his ar [...]

Ra

Contir [...]
Alrea [...]
charge [...]
having [...]
be wi [...]
chary [...]
[...]
his y [...]

Lackner's murder trial relocated

By VALERI OLIVER
Tribune Staff Writer

INVERNESS — Ronald Paul Lackner earned a change of venue to Lake County Monday, where he will stand trial on a first-degree murder charge in the shooting death of his ex-wife.

Lackner, 36, requested a change of venue from Citrus County because of publicity concerning the charge against him in connection with the death of Mary Lackner, 32, whose body was discovered in her mobile home near Inglis July 3.

The trial has been set for Dec. 14 in Lake County.

In arguing for the change of venue, Assistant Public Defender Charles Vaughn said, "We feel that there has been too much press coverage of this trial."

...tate Attorney Brad

during a September hearing ...ff's investigator said Lac... ...mitted he shot Mary Lack... by mistake and twice m... she asked to be put out o... ...ery.

Sgt. Bruce Lovett tes... Lackner told officials th... to his ex-wife's home a... ...ment ensued. Lackner ... shot the woman in th... then agreed to kill he... asked to be put out of ... according to testimony.

The Baldwin Times
"The greatest good for the greatest number"

Council names new police chief
Bruce Lovett of Inverness, Fla., chosen at stormy Tuesday meeting

Deputy leaves for Alabama department

Citrus sheriff's investigator accepts police chief position

Bloody shooting in Bay Minette leaves two dead

By GUY BUSBY
and DAVE PARKER
Press Register Reporters

BAY MINETTE, Ala. — Most people in area shops, offices and the Courthouse were waiting for the electrical power to come back on or for lunchtime to come around when two rifle shots rifle echoed through downtown Bay Minette Monday.

Sandra Sirmon Gladrosich, 34, of Pine Grove and her mother, Ruby Smith Cobb, 55, of Repton, Ala., had been fatally wounded in the parking lot of a downtown law office at around 11:45 a.m.

Mrs. Gladrosich's estranged husband, Raymond Gladrosich, 37, was arrested a few minutes later driving north on Hoyle Avenue, a few blocks from where the shooting occurred.

Attorney Bayless Biles said the Gladrosiches had come to his office to discuss their divorce. The attorney said he was told by the couple that there was no problem with the ending of the marriage agreed to the

they disagreed about was the four children and he agreed to give them back to her."

Biles said Mrs. Cobb remained in the waiting room during the meeting. The attorney said that few minutes after the three left, heard the shots in the parking l

"I'm totally in shock," Biles sai "When I had talked to them the wasn't any reason to believe an thing like this was going to ha pen."

The shooting, on U.S. High 31 a block east of the Courthou also shocked the many work who ran out to investigate sounds and saw a man standing the lot with a rifle.

The electricity was out in part of Bay Minette and so people in the area first thought sounds were connected with power failure.

One man, who asked not to identified, said he was eating lu when the shooting occurred. of a sudden I heard this bang a thought the transformer blown out," he said. "When I ed out, it was all over. He was

Two slain in Bay Minette

Husband of victim charged with murder

By SUZY PARKER
and GUY BUSBY
Press Register Reporters

Paramedics and police in Bay Minette prepare to carry a victim to an ambulance following Monday's double shooting. Sandra Sirmon Giadrosich, 34, of Pine Grove, and her mother, Ruby Smith Cobb, 55, of Repton, Ala., were pronounced dead at North Baldwin Hospital after the shootings.

See SLAYING, 6A, Col. 1

Giadrosich told police chief he shot wife, mother-in-law

By Paige Ponder
Staff Writer

Bay Minette Police Chief Bruce Lovett said at a preliminary hearing that Raymond Eugene Giadrosich told him that he had shot his wife and mother-in-law minutes after a street shooting Aug. 5 in Bay Minette.

Following the preliminary hearing Aug. 8, the 37-year-old Giadrosich of Bay Minette was bound over to a Baldwin County grand jury in the shooting deaths of his wife and mother-in-law. District Court Judge Pamela Baschab determined there was probable cause to believe that Giadrosich committed the murders with which he has been charged.

At about 11:45 a.m. Aug. 5, Sandra Sirmon Giadrosich of Bay Minette and Ruby Smith Cobb of Repton were shot and killed outside the law offices of Wilkins, Bankester, Biles and Wynne on East Second Street in Bay Minette. The women were shot moments after the Giadrosiches had left the office where they had been discussing the terms of a divorce.

Bay Minette Police Chief Bruce Lovett said he was patrolling the area Monday approximately six blocks from the shooting scene when he heard what he thought were two gunshots. Driving toward the sound, he looked for anyone leaving the scene in a hurry or acting strangely. He stopped Giadrosich because he was leaving the scene and could have possibly been a witness.

Giadrosich asked Lovett if he knew where the Baldwin County Sheriff's Department was and when Lovett identified himself as the chief of police, Giadrosich said, "I just shot my wife and

See Giadrosich, Page 6A

197

Taylor capital murder case goes to grand ju[ry]

By Graham Heath
Staff Writer

A Baldwin County grand jury will hear evidence against a Bay Minette man charged with murder in connection with the brutal beating death of an elderly Bay Minette man on Christmas Day 1996.

After more than an hour of testimony Monday involving Robert Taylor, 34, District Judge Langford Floyd found there was probable cause and turned the case over to the grand jury for consideration.

Taylor is accused of capital murder in the death of Moody Knight, 75, who was found beaten, cold and near death inside his residence where he lived alone. He had been gagged with a pair of brown socks and his arms were tied behind him with tennis shoe laces. He died at the hospital the following morning.

During testimony at the Monday hearing, Sgt. Roland [...], a criminal [...]

doesn't show he (Taylor) is g[...] It just shows he was near [...] scene."

currently in prison, atta[...] Knight and left the resi[...] with money, a pocket knife [...] some keys.

On Monday, Crook said T[...] had said he followed the [...] man to the house but did [...] know what was going to happ[...]

However, Taylor's statem[...] that he remained outside [...] house are inconsistent with [...] finding of Knight's blood on [...] shoes.

Crook said Knight wore a pa[...] over one eye and used a cane [...] lowing a stroke. He said Kni[...] had been beaten with the c[...] and kicked, leaving him brui[...] and bloody. Crook added t[...] some blood was found on a c[...] peted area of the house, but fo[...] prints were impossible to lift.

The genetic traits of blo[...] found on the tongue of the [...] shoe occurs in [...] 500 [...]

"The greatest good [...]

[a]nd operated   Thursday, J[...]

Guilty as charged!

[J]ury returns McCant[s] [v]erdict within 2 hour[s]

[R]oselle Zayas
[W]riter

[BA]Y MINETTE — After one and a-half hours of deliberat[ions,] [a Baldw]in County jury rendered a verdict of guilty in the case a[gainst] [Antho]ny Terrell McCants.

[Mc]Cants, 33, of Bay Minette, was found guilty of all 15 co[unts] [of ch]arges on which he was indicted, including four counts of [...] [...] burglary, three counts of first degree burglary, one o[...]

See McCants, Pa[ge ...]

The Baldwin Times

"The greatest good for the greatest number"

Thursday, January 9, 1997   Bay Minette, Alabama • 50 Cents

McCants trial under way

By Rozelle Zayas
Of Times

More than two years after a series of burglaries and rapes in the Bay Minette and Pine Grove communities, suspect Anthony Terrell McCants now faces a Baldwin County jury.

McCants, 33, has been accused of multiple counts of rapes, robberies and rapes in connection with the series brought me to both communities.

The circuit court case deals with the incidents including the burglaries of the homes of seven women during a spree of burglaries between May 1993 and August 1994, ... of the women's cases involve burglaries only. The ... or cases involve rape, robbery and burglary.

After a day and a half of jury selection, attorneys provided opening arguments and began witness testimony Baldwin County Presiding Circuit Judge Charles ... in a courtroom Tuesday afternoon.

... within County District Attorney David Whetstone ... the attorneys had managed to qualify 34 jurors for the trial by the end of the day Monday. Whetstone said he had expected to begin proceedings on Wednesday.

However, the trial is expected to take some time.

"This is a case that will be technical," Whetstone said. Whetstone said he plans to present each piece of evidence as part of a puzzle, and to go along on the actual ...

Part of the evidence expected to be introduced during the trial includes DNA evidence. That was one area McCants' attorney, William Scully, addressed during his opening statement.

The defense attorney explained in detail to the jurors as to how the present works, while citing the possibility of scientist error while trying to find a match.

"How do you know," he said, "They might not be exactly alike."

Scully also alluded to an earlier arrest investigators made during the case of another suspect, warning that it is a "pretty serious mistake to put a man away on DNA evidence."

One of the first witnesses to testify during Tuesday's proceedings was Lt. Huey "Gus" Mack Jr., chief investigator with the Baldwin County Sheriff's Department.

Mack testified regarding the collection of fingerprints from some of the scenes, as well as photographs of the homes of a number of the victims and a phone of McCants' automobile.

During cross examination Scully asked the investigator which sets of fingerprints he had lifted and how many. Mack said he lifted nine sets from one woman, three sets from another, four from a third and eight from a fourth victim.

The defendant's automobile was also the subject of an October 1994 search that the investigator testified about despite objections from Scully.

Scully objected to the admissibility of the evidence found during the search of McCants' car.

However, Perrin overruled the defense's objection.

Mack also testified in court that at the time of search, McCants had already been arrested.

See McCants, Page

...tle to ...arved

Lovett vice president of chiefs association

By Joanna Bailey
Of Times

Bay Minette Police Chief Bruce ...tt was recently elected vice president of the Alabama Association of Chiefs of Police, first time anyone from Baldwin County has been elected either the vice president or president's post.

The association, which was ...ded in 1970 and now has ...ximately 200 members, is ...ved in addressing statewide ... pertaining to proposed ... legislation and issues ... relating to police officers and ... chiefs in the state.

... vice president of the association ...t, Lovett will be a member of ... board of directors.

...ording to AACOP's executive ...or Gloria ..., Lovett will fill

Chief Bruce Lovett

...in the absence of the association's president. He will periodically travel to Montgomery to ...

See "Lovett," Page 11A

---

the greatest number"

Bay Minette, Alabama • 50 Cents

Lovett taped for 'Court TV'

Staff Report

Former Bay Minette Police Chief Bruce Lovett will be one of several investigators highlighted Saturday in a "Court TV" segment involving a kidnapping and murder case.

The documentary will be broadcast at 9 p.m.

Lovett headed the Citrus County, Fla., Sheriff's general investigation department in 1988 during the time of the investigation.

Lovett said he and other investigators returned to Florida earlier this year to meet with producers for about a week and tape the segments.

Lovett retired from law enforcement after a 33-year career.

LOVETT

Federal Bureau of Investigations (FBI)
Director, Louis Freeh

CPSIA information can be obtained
at www.ICGtesting.com
Printed in the USA
FFHW021343200319
51168003-56627FF